Greetings from Pittsburgh
A Picture Postcard History

by Ralph Ashworth

The Vestal Press, Ltd.
Vestal, New York

Library of Congress Cataloging-in-Publication Data

Ashworth, Ralph, 1951-
    Greetings from Pittsburgh : a picture postcard history / by Ralph Ashworth
        p. cm.
    Includes bibliographical references.
    ISBN 0-911572-98-8 (pbk. : A-free) : $11.95
    1. Pittsburgh (Pa.)--Pictorial works. 2. Postcards--Pennsylvania--Pittsburgh.
    I. Title
    F159.P643A84 1992
    974.8'86041'0222--dc20   92-15450
                                                                              CIP

Printed in the United States of America

Cover design by Don Bell

Vestal Press Picture Postcard titles include

Cornell and Ithaca in Postcards by Harvey N. Roehl
Old Milwaukee: A Historic Tour in Picture Postcards by Gregory Filardo
Oklahoma, A Land and Its People: Early Views and History in Picture Postcards by Jack H. Smith
Philadelphia in Early Picture Postcards, 1900-1930 by Philip Jamison III
Railroads in Early Postcards Vol. 1: Upstate New York by Richard Palmer and Harvey Roehl
Railroads in Early Postcards Vol 2: Northern New England by Stephen Boothroyd and Peter Barney
Where's the Fire? American Firefighters in Picture Postcards circa 1910 by Geoffrey N. Stein
Cleveland in Picture Postcards, 1900-1930 by Ralph Burnham Thompson
Greetings from Pittsburgh: A Picture Postcard History by Ralph Ashworth

Write for a catalogue listing our other fine books.

The Vestal Press, Ltd.
PO Box 97
Vestal, NY 13851-0097

Introduction

One day upon entering one of my favorite book stores I noticed a squarish tin on the counter. The tin held a hundred or so peculiar-looking postcards.

"Antique postcards," the manager told me. "We're going to start selling them in the store."

This was the innocent beginning of an intensive, eight-year project that resulted in the book you now hold in your hands. I just couldn't keep away from that tin! There was the card showing Lake Elizabeth, for instance. Who would have thought there was, at one time, a lake in West Park that was large enough for swimming laps and located on the very grounds where my cousin and I used to play while wating for the Garden or Kenyon Theater to open? I had to have that card. And, as a jazz fan, I had to have the card of the old Casino nightclub in the Hill District. And here was a picture of the Bijou Theater and Sixth Street, submerged in three feet of water. Duquesne Gardens — where was that? Oakland? None of my friends knew anything about or even remembered what went on at Duquesne Gardens. Why was it torn down? Curious, I went to the Pennsylvania Room at the Carnegie Library and read through old newspaper clippings — some were actually reviews of events that had transpired at the Gardens. I learned that opera had been a big hit at the Gardens; Caruso had begged to play there. The Ice Capades were introduced to the world at the Gardens. Hockey was so popular at the Gardens that four hockey teams played there on a regular basis; in fact, professional hockey was born at the Gardens.

When I returned my folder of clippings to the librarian, I asked, "How many more of these folders of clippings do you have on Pittsburgh history?"

She pointed to two long rows of metal filing cabinets.

"And there's more on microfiche," she said.

I thought of all the cards that I had collected so far. As a writer, I knew well enough how little of Pittsburgh's popular, or social, history had been preserved in book form. There it all was — in old tattered clippings printed on newspaper so highly fragile that much of it crumbled at a touch. That was when I got the idea for this book.

It would be helpful to understand a little of the history of postcard collecting. Just before the turn of the century, the United States postal service approved the use of unsealed cards for mail delivery. This enabled someone to send a short message ("Arrived safely in Pittsburgh") instead of a full-fleged letter. It didn't take long for people to want to send a card that contained a picture (say, of Pittsburgh) along with that message. At first, the postal service would not permit a message to be written on the address side of a postal card. For this reason, postcard manufacturers allowed a small margin at the bottom or side of the card's picture for scribbling in a message. This is why some of the cards shown in this book have writing on the front of the card. Within a relatively short time, the postal service agreed to allow postcard customers to put their mesesage on the back along with the mailing address. This freed up the entire front of the card for photography or artwork.

For the first time in history, it was possible, for very little money, to collect pictures of one's hometown or places far away. This initiated a postcard-collecting mania. The Germans developed a process for hand-tinting the postcards so that they could be printed in color. For this reason, many of the cards dating from this early period state that that they were manufactured in Germany. Postcard collecting remained a popular fad until World War I put an end to German postcard production. After the war, people still colelcted postcards, just as they do today, but it was never quite the same. This period from the inception of the postcard until World War I is considered the Golden Age of postcard collecting. This is why so many of the cards in collectible shops, and most of the cards presented in this book, date from that early period.

However, I like the postcards for the glimpse that they offer of the past. As I took my cards to the Pennsylvania Room and researched the history behind each one, a different picture of Pittsburgh emerged for me. I have thought of Pittsburgh as a conservative city, a place of calculated moves and measured risks. It was interesting for me to see how outrageous we once were — gamblers, pirates, and high-stakes operators. We filled burlesque houses, charged through the streets with rifles and pistols, canoed our way to work during floods, held funerals in theaters with tens of thousands of people in attendance, and lined the streets to send our soldiers off to war.

I came to appreciate our boldness as a people, our resourcefulness, above all our sense of amusement, our sense of fun. Today when I walk through our downtown streets, I see the giant skyscrapers of modern Pittsburgh, but I also see the ghosts of our past. When I walk past the Benedum Center, I see the old Stanley Theater where master of ceremonies Dick Powell introduced a young Burns and Allen. When I walk past a nondescript parking garage along the Boulevard of the Allies, I see the old log school building that became the first institution of higher learning in Western Pennsylvania. When I walk across our aging Smithfield Street Bridge, I see pleasure boats on the Mon; but I also see the location from which lookouts spotted a barge full of Pinkerton agents on their way up the river to Homestead. The city is more alive for me now that I know of its past. Looking through these old postcards, I feel my heritage as a Pittsburgher.

My goal in writing this book is to share the excitement that I felt at discovering this other Pittsburgh through my collection of cards. I have interviewed many people who remember the old days, and I have extensively researched information that has heretofore not been published in book form. Undoubtedly, a date or two has been misappropriated along the way — that much is inevitable — but I assure you that every outlandish thing published in this book is true; both I and the *Pittsburgh Sun Telegraph* of 1909 are prepared to stand behind it.

Best wishes,
Ralph Ashworth

Pittsburgh

    This lithograph by artist William Schuchman shows the view from Coal Hill (Mount Washington). The wedge of land that was Pittsburgh proper, nicely delineated here, came to be known as The Golden Triangle because of the tremendous amount of business transacted within it. When this lithograph was done in 1858 , Pittsburgh produced about $50,000,000 worth of manufactured goods and was known as The Iron City. This is one of the very few historic "maps" of Pittsburgh ever issued as a postcard.

Block House, Pittsburgh, Pa.

In 1753, young George Washington wrote in his journal that the Point (then called the Fork) was "extremely well situated for a Fort, as it has the Command of both rivers." Both the English and the French claimed possession of the strategic Ohio Valley area. A group of Virginians representing the English built the first fort at the Point. A larger group of Frenchmen ordered the Virginians to abandon their fort. The French then constructed Fort Duquesne. In 1758 the English general John Forbes forced the French to abandon their fort. Forbes then ordered the erection of Fort Pitt, named in honor of English Prime Minister William Pitt.

The Block House shown here was built in 1764 to strengthen Fort Pitt's western flank against flood damage. It is all that remains of Fort Pitt. The Block House is the oldest building in the Golden Triangle.

Point Bridge and Exposition Buildings at Junction of Ohio, Allegheny and Monongahela Rivers, Pittsburg, Pa.

24798

Exposition centers like this one provided a permanent showcase for local business and industry. The first Pittsburgh area exposition opened in Allegheny City along the North Shore in 1875. It burned to the ground in 1883. In 1885, the Western Pennsylvania Exposition Society was incorporated to develop a permanent facility that would promote Pittsburgh's industrial innovations. The city leased the grounds at The Point for a dollar a year, stipulating that school children attend free of charge. The new Western Pennsylvania Exposition, pictured here, opened in 1889.

Western Pennsylvania Exposition Bld'g's, Pittsburgh, Pa.

The large structure in the foreground is the Main Exposition Building; in the center is the Music Hall; and next is Machinery Hall with a foundry on one floor, a machine shop on the other, and galleries on each side. This last building could be disassembled and reassembled at will—even the slate roof was held on with removable copper nails. Machinery Hall held exhibits of specific goods offered by Pittsburgh manufacturers. The Main Exposition Building held industrial and commercial exhibits; in 1898, these included a state-of-the-art Pullman Car display and a dazzling Westinghouse demonstration of the practical uses of their new alternating-current electrical scheme.

There was talk of using the Exposition Society's profits to build a polytechnical institute in Pittsburgh where the sons of Pittsburgh's laborers could be educated at minimal cost to take their place in the industrial world of the future. Andrew Carnegie liked this idea so much that he created the Carnegie Technical Schools.

This is a look at the inside of the Main building. Displays for the Rosenbaum Co., Campbell's Soups, and H. J. Heinz can be seen by looking closely.

Ice skating and roller skating were enormously popular pastimes early in this century. Here is a picture of choreographed roller skating in the Main building.

The stated purpose of the Exposition's Music Hall was to promote musical events of high cultural value (as opposed to vaudeville's low cultural value). John Philip Sousa, Victor Herbert, and Walter Damrosch with his New York Symphony were among the musicians who performed there. Stage plays and silent movies were also offered.

SEASON 1916-1917   WINTER GARDEN
PITTSBURGH   EXPOSITION BUILDING

The back of this Exposition advertising card from the 1916-1917 season reads: "Meet me at the Winter Garden, Tuesday Evening November 21st. MONSTER ICE CARNIVAL." Regretfully, no expositions were held after the U. S. entered World War I. By 1919, the society's debts were staggering, the grounds and buildings were in serious disrepair, and there was no interest in staging an exposition after the war. The city assumed the Society's debts and took over the buildings. Music Hall, which was left to rot, was demolished in 1941. Machinery Hall, used for a time by the Pittsburgh Railway Company as a trolley station, was demolished in 1942. The Main Building became an auto pound and fell to the wrecking ball in 1951 to clear ground for Point State Park.

This was Pittsburgh's first incline; it still runs today as a tourist attraction to take visitors up to the Mount Washington bluff where The Golden Triangle and surrounding hills can be viewed. Built in 1870 by John J. Endres, it was designed primarily to accommodate pedestrians (tracks with small cars on the right). In 1883, the freight incline was added (tracks on the left). These tracks are 640 feet long with a rise of 375 feet and run from Carson Street at the bottom to Grandview Avenue, Mount Washington, at the top. The Pittsburgh and Lake Erie Railroad's freight house can be seen in the lower right corner of the picture.

Looking Down Castle Shannon Incline,
South Side, Pittsburg, Pa.

Pittsburgh is bound on the north and south by grand hillsides and steep slopes. As the city's industry and population expanded, the incline evolved as the most practical way to get people from the city to the suburbs. At one time, there were seventeen inclines in operation. This one was owned by the Pittsburgh and Castle Shannon Railroad Co., and ran from East Carson Street at the bottom to Bailey Avenue, Mount Washington, from 1890 to 1964.

The Eleventh Street Incline was the city's second curved incline. It outlasted most other inclines and was widely traveled. Built by J. H. McRoberts in 1890, it ran from Eleventh Street on the South Side to Warrington and Arlington Avenues in Knoxville — a distance of 2,640 feet. Rails on the Eleventh Street end were elevated bridge-style. After progressing 980 feet, the incline leveled onto solid ground. As seen here, it was designed to carry horses and their freight, as well as people. The Twelfth Street Incline can be seen in the background. The first curved incline was built on the North Side and ran from Federal Street up to Nunnery Hill in Fineview.

Eleventh Street Incline, S. S. Pittsburgh, Pa.

Duquesne Incline, S. S. Pittsburg, Pa.

The Duquesne Passenger Incline was built by Samuel Diescher in 1877 on the steep hillside across from The Point. It was 780 feet long with a rise of 400 feet. When it looked as if this incline would be put out of service, a group of concerned citizens formed the Society for the Preservation of the Duquesne Heights Incline in order to save it. The station at the bottom of the tracks is still as it was at the turn of the century; the original wooden cars from 1877 have been restored. A ride on the Duquesne Incline is one of the premiere tourist attractions in Pittsburgh.

This "temple of grandeur and comfort," the Pittsburgh Opera House, opened in 1871 to offer the finest attractions in legitimate and stock theater. It was Pittsburgh's first "carriage trade" theater. In 1905, a fire destroyed much of it. It reopened as The Grand, offering vaudeville from early in the morning until midnight. Performers included Eddie Cantor, nine-year-old Georgie Jessel, and Will Rogers. In 1917, another fire destroyed the Grand's auditorium. This time it re-opened as The Million Dollar Grand, a cinema house. Instead of the usual organ off to the side, the ritzy Grand had a full orchestra off stage to accompany Valentino's love scenes. Years later, the theater was sold to the Warner Theater chain and became The Warner. In 1953, the Warner's interior was rebuilt to accommodate the new Cinerama process. In 1983, the Warner closed its doors; the building is now an office/retail complex.

Sixth Street and Penn Avenue, Under Four Feet of Water
Greatest flood ever recorded in ——eny county, Monongahela river guaging 36.2 ft. of water, and Allegheny river 36.6 ft. Next greatest flood, the celebr   "in Flood" of 1832, followed by the 1884 flood, which was 3.3 ft. less.

The flood of 1907 inspired postcards showing streets that were otherwise uninteresting to postcard collectors. This is Sixth Street from Liberty Avenue; the Sixth Street Bridge is in the far background. By using a magnifying glass, two of the city's oldest theaters can be seen: the Bijou and the Alvin. The Bijou was part of Library Hall (there was for many years a library on the second floor of the building). The notorious Mrs. Lilly Langtry played Pittsburgh here. Library Hall and its theater were torn down after the flood of 1936.

The Alvin was named after the main character of a "farmer comedy" titled Alvin Joslyn, written by Charles Lindsay Davis. He made a fortune on the East Coast after opening his play in Pittsburgh in 1879. After retirement, he opened The Alvin. Later, Samuel Nixon owned the theater for about ten years before he opened The Nixon; even later, the famous Shubert company bought it and changed the name to the Shubert-Alvin, remodelling it in the Art Deco style. The theater remained popular until the roof collapsed — chandelier first — during a matinee presentation. The theater later reopened as The Gateway. The building currently houses a health and fitness club.

According to John Barhart, master electrician, theater entrepreneur Samuel Nixon built The Nixon to be "the finest theater in the world, with the best of everything in it." Costing over $1,000,000 to build in 1903, it featured an 87 x 47-foot stage (the largest stage in legitimate theater for as long as the Nixon stood), 32 backstage dressing rooms arranged in five tiers, and a gradually sloping walkway to the balcony instead of a stairway. On opening night, Thomas Kirk, the Nixon's general manager, drove his electric car up this promenade. Opening night tickets to see Lillian Russell, Gay Nineties idol and native Pittsburgher, were auctioned for charity. No favoritism was shown: Senator George T. Oliver paid $500 for his — the price of a small farm. Miss Russell's photograph set off the famous "Rogue's Gallery" looking down from the backstage that included John and Ethel Barrymore, Helen Hayes, Sarah Bernhardt, George M. Cohan, Sophie Tucker, Fanny Brice, and Katharine Hepburn. Florenz Ziegfeld premiered most of his "Follies" at the Nixon. Because Pittsburgh audiences were known to be cold, Ziegfeld said that if the show was a hit at the Nixon, it could be a hit anywhere.

308 Nixon Theatre, Pittsburg, Pa.

This card shows a later, altered ground floor window treatment. To the left of the new window was the entrance to the Nixon Cafe where Pittsburghers could hobnob with the stars. Unusual for 1903, the Nixon had its own electrical power supply. During the flood of 1907, most of downtown Pittsburgh was without electricity. Since The Nixon was above the flood line and had its own power supply, Sam Nixon decided that the show would go on. Pittsburghers canoed their way through four feet of water to the newly created Smithfield Street dock in order to see the latest Lillian Russell play. Mae West closed the Nixon in 1950 with her revival of Diamond Lil. The theater was demolished soon afterwards.

Nixon Theatre, Pittsburg, Pa.

The beautiful Beaux-Arts architecture of the Nixon was rare for Pittsburgh. This street panorama shows the Nixon in its architectural context, alongside building styles more typical for Pittsburgh.

This card from the early 1930's is an artist's rendering of the Stanley Theater, one of three multi-million dollar movie palaces built in Pittsburgh in 1927 (the others were the Enright, in East Liberty, and the Loews-Penn, downtown). This theater cost over $3,000,000 to build and was part of a $10,000,000 complex that included the Clark building. Opening night featured the silent original of *Gentlemen Prefer Blondes* and The Stanley Chorus—not a bevy of lovely women with shapely legs, but thirty burly men dressed up in industrial costumes. The Stanley offered live shows along with movies. Dick Powell was the master of ceremonies for three years before moving on to Hollywood. The Marx Brothers performed at the Stanley, as did Burns and Allen, Mickey Rooney, Martin and Lewis, Judy Garland, Nat King Cole, and Frank Sinatra. This theater was restored in the 1980's and re-christened The Benedum Center For The Performing Arts.

Market House, Pittsburg, Pa.

In 1784, the Penn family deeded the stretch of land now called Market Square to the people of Pittsburgh. City fathers designed the land for use as a public square. Retailers, farmers, bakers, and butchers established themselves at stalls or in wooden buildings around the perimeter. The Market House pictured here was one of two similar structures built in the 1850's. The one on the east side of Market Street was called, logically enough, East Market House; the one on the west side was called West Market House. During the Civil War, East Market House was used as a residence and hospital for Union soldiers. Both buildings were destroyed by fire early in this century. Displaced farmers moved to a makeshift market along Duquesne Way (now Fort Duquesne Blvd.) while the city looked into creating a new market house.

MARKET ST.
PITTSBURG, PA.

This is a relatively rare postcard of Market Street as it looked in 1907.

City fathers authorized a massive H-shape structure for a new Market House that closed the open public square for the first time in Pittsburgh history. The Diamond Market House was a red brick building designed by the Pittsburgh architecture firm Alden and Harlow. It opened in 1915 with many stalls for farmers, butchers, and bakers plus an exhibition hall and a sporting ring. Boxing became a popular attraction at this Market House.

The view on this linen card shows the south side of the market looking down Market Street to Liberty Avenue. The connecting walkway between the two buildings hovered above Diamond Street. The Market House was designed so that Diamond Street ran through the two buildings, thus allowing it to remain open to traffic. This Market House was demolished with a great deal of controversy in the early 1960's. Renaissance I, a program to modernize and beautify The Golden Triangle, deemed that the land originally deeded by the Penns would look more attractive as an open square.

This rare card shows the downtown river front along the Allegheny River approaching The Point. Industrialist Henry Phipps purchased and developed this land. The three skyscrapers are (left to right) the Fulton Building (still standing), the Bessemer Building, and the Natatorium. The first two were office buildings. The Natatorium began as the Duquesne Athletic Club, an exclusive men's club. It reorganized in 1909 as the Pittsburgh Natatorium, a less exclusive swimming and bathing facility that provided a healthful alternative for area children who would otherwise have had to swim in the disease-plagued rivers. No expense was spared in creating the Natatorium's lavish, palatial interior; only the finest Italian marble was used.

Allegheny River Front, showing Duquesne Market, Fulton, Bessemer and Natatorium Buildings, Pittsburgh, Pa.

To the left of the Fulton Building is one of Pittsburgh's oldest live theaters, the Gayety. Entertainment here leaned toward the lighter side, vaudeville and burlesque primarily. Across the street and in front of these buildings is the Duquesne Market, a makeshift open market created after fire destroyed the East and West Market Houses.

A rare interior view of the Natatorium. Note the elaborate brickwork of the arched ceiling. This photograph must have been taken during a swim meet or special competition. Hats were in vogue back then. Every woman wore a hat to a social event. Men usually sported bowler hats but took them off indoors.

The Pittsburgh chapter of the Y. M. C. A. was the fifth in the nation when founded in 1854. The organization operated out of church space and rented rooms for many years. This wonderful Queen Anne-style building, erected 1883-1884, was on the corner of Seventh and Penn where the Benedum Center stands today. It was Pittsburgh's first Central Y. This facility stirred up a bit of controversy when it first opened because the first floor and basement were gymnasiums, considered the exclusive domain of prize fighters and riff-raff at that time. Before long, however, this Y and others across the country were able to demonstrate the contribution that teamwork and athletic skills made to the moral character of young men. The first basketball and volleyball games in Pittsburgh were played at this Y. This building was eventually abandoned for a larger facility on Wood Street and was demolished in the mid-1920's.

MONONGAHELA HOUSE, PITTSBURGH

The Monongahela House was built in 1839-1840 on the corner of Smithfield and Water Street (Fort Pitt Blvd.) within spitting distance of the Mon Wharf. In those days, Pittsburgh was the busiest inland port-of-call in the nation with hundreds of river vessels docking at the wharf each week. This first-class facility, considered the finest hotel west of the Allegheny Mountains, served Charles Dickens, Jenny Lind, and P. T. Barnum. President-elect Abraham Lincoln delivered a speech to the citizens of Pittsburgh from the hotel's balcony. Unfortunately, various forms of inland transportation eventually rendered the hotel's wharfside location less of an asset. Newer first-class hotels with more modern facilities stole its business. In the 1920's, major renovations brought elevators, a new cafeteria, and enhanced entertainment facilities such as a larger billiard area and bowling lanes; but to no avail. The Monongahela House closed its doors in 1935.

This is how the Mon Wharf would have looked on a typical day in 1902, the date printed on this card. Paddle steamers had revolutionized Pittsburgh river traffic. The Victorian buildings in the background ran along Water Street (Fort Pitt Blvd.). Many of these buildings still stand today. The Monongahela House was up the street to the right.

The photograph for this card was taken on the afternoon of the River Parade during the Sesqui-centennial celebration of 1908. The parade, which chronicled the evolution of riverboat traffic during Pittsburgh's first 150 years, featured a fleet of 50 steam boats, including a replica of the *New Orleans*, the first steamboat to travel in these waters.

This is how the Monongahela River would have looked on any day during Pittsburgh's reign as a great industrial center. Here we see steamboats, towboats, and coal barges.

COAL FLEET AWAITING HIGH WATER STAGE FOR SHIPMENT TO THE SOUTH, PITTSBURG, PA.

Before the advent of the lock-and-dam system, rivers were filled from shore to shore with boats waiting for high water. If the weather was uncooperative, boatmen could be stuck in Pittsburgh for months. In the background is the Wabash Bridge, which led into the Wabash Station.

The rivers around Pittsburgh are not particularly deep. In the dry season, traffic on the rivers could be held up for months. At best, the rivers were full of rocks and trees, and riddled with shoals that produced eddies, cross currents, and short rapids known as "ripples" or "riffles." In the 1700's and early 1800's, boatmen built "wingwalls" — boulders placed in the river in a V-shape to channel water to a center lane through which boats could then pass. These wingwalls were built and maintained by boatmen on a volunteer basis. Later, the State of Pennsylvania granted a charter to a group of private citizens to create a series of locks and dams along the Monongahela River. This group, The Monongahela Navigation Company, opened Lock No. 1 about a mile above the Smithfield Street Bridge in 1841. A series of four locks and dams were in operation

Lock No. 1, Monongahela River, Pittsburg, Pa.

on the Mon by 1844. Riverboat traffic increased enormously once the rivers could be navigated year round, and a second lock was built at Lock No. 1 beside the first one to accommodate larger coal barges. Toward the end of the 19th century, opposition to the tolls of The Monongahela Navigation Company was so great that the company was forced to sell its assets. The U. S. government acquired the Monongahela lock-and-dam systems in 1897.

Davis Island Dam and Lock, Pittsburgh, Pa.

In the 1800's, the obstacles that boatmen encountered were actually named and mapped. Cow Island and Horsetail Ripple, two such spots, were located close together about five miles down the Ohio river from The Point. As early as 1824, the Army Corps of Engineers worked to clear the Ohio of rocks and fallen trees that made travel in the Ohio River difficult. After the Civil War, the Corps worked on managing the water levels on the river. In 1878, the U. S. government purchased a portion of Cow Island from the Davis family (who grazed cows there; hence, its name), and the land became Davis Island. The Corps built the first lock and moveable dam on the Ohio here in 1885.

Pittsburg, Pa., Coal Boats at Point Bridge.

John Roebling popularized the suspension bridge in Pittsburgh. This card shows the Point Suspension Bridge of 1877. The design by Edward Himberle was considered unique. Eight-inch eye-bar cables were drawn through 110-foot iron towers. The cables then formed a bowstring truss, which joined together at the center of the bridge from each side. It was somewhat awkward-looking but did the job. Unfortunately, it had not been designed with the automobile in mind. The Point Suspension Bridge was replaced with another type of bridge in the late 1920's.

First Presbyterian Church,
Sixth Avenue, Pittsburg, Pa

In the 1780's, Hugh Henry Brackenridge, Pittsburgh's first statesman, pushed the state legislature to establish a non-sectarian church in Pittsburgh. However, the Scots-Irish, who dominated the population at that time, saw to it that this state-sanctioned church became Presbyterian. The first church building was made of logs and fronted on Virgin Alley. A second church made of brick was built in 1802. Some records suggest that this brick church was built around the original log church, which was then burned out from within. Population growth necessitated the creation of yet a third church building. This cut stone structure, erected on Wood Street in 1853, was similar to the one that stands today.

Toward the end of the century industrialist Henry Oliver purchased much of the land in the Sixth and Wood Street area. He decided that the Wood Street location of the 1853 church was better suited for development.

The building pictured on this postcard was built on Sixth Street, just around the corner from the old Wood Street location, between 1903-1905. It features a Geneva Pulpit between the front stairways. Outdoor (or Geneva) pulpits date back to the Reformation when sermons were delivered to the masses in the street. In the 1930's Reverend Dr. Clarence Macartney condemned Darwin's theory of evolution from this pulpit. On one occasion a rival "modernist" pastor pointed out that the stone in Dr. Macartney's pulpit was made of ancient marine fossils that proved Darwin's theory of evolution to be correct.

This card contrasts the Gothic elegance of the Presbyterian Church with the McCreery Building — the structure Henry Oliver erected on the site of the earlier Wood Street church.

In 1849, 23-year-old Joseph Horne opened his first shop on Market Street near Fourth Avenue in a small, three-story, wooden-framed building. The retail and wholesale stock was described in Horne's first newspaper ad as "trimmings and fancy goods." The next year, Horne expanded into umbrellas, imported goods, and men's furnishings. A popular item in the woman's clothing department was the hoop skirt. During his years on Market Street, Joseph Horne created the special service of home delivery — made in a wheelbarrow. In 1871, Joseph Horne & Co. moved to the larger Library Hall on Penn Avenue where Horne's became known as a special-order dress shop. Every year, Horne's buyer made a trip to Paris, took in the latest fashions, and adapted what he saw for the Pittsburgh market. In 1893, the store moved into its own building at Penn and Stanwix Street. This six-story structure burned down to its steel frame four years later. The store was rebuilt and expanded to the size pictured at the top of this advertising card.

This card, postmarked 1908, shows Pittsburgh's old City Hall. This elegant French Renaissance building, designed by Pittsburgh architect Joseph W. Kerr, opened in 1872. The entrance faced Smithfield Street and occupied the lot where Saks Fifth Avenue stands today. The official time of the clock tower was precisely set by the Allegheny Observatory. The domed belfry above the clock tower contained a two-ton bell that rang out the hour and was part of the city's fire alarm system. Pittsburgh's municipal offices moved to the City County Building on Grant Street in 1917. Although used for secondary office space, this structure languished until its demolition in 1953.

Pittsburg Post Office, Pittsburg, Pa.

This post office dates from a time when the architecture department of the government was committed to design quality and beauty. The plans for this particular structure were prepared by M. E. Bell. It was erected on Smithfield Street between Third and Fourth Street in 1892. The exterior was of Vermont granite while the interior featured marble and slate from Vermont, Tennessee, and Kentucky as well as mahogany from Africa. The Post Office Department occupied the first floor of the building; and upper floors were used by the Federal Courts, the Internal Revenue Service, and the U. S. Attorney, among others. In 1934, a larger, more modern post office was built on Seventh and Grant. Other federal offices, including military recruiting offices, remained in this building until the Federal Building went up on Liberty and Grant. This building is gone now.

Smithfield St. from Third Ave., Looking North. Federal Building on Right, Pittsburgh, Pa.

This photographic card was published by the Union News Company of New York and Pittsburgh. Everyone in this picture is wearing a hat. Note the policeman on the street in front of the trolley, who is wearing white gloves and an English bobbie-style hat. Note also the cobblestone streets—almost every street in Pittsburgh was paved with cobblestone. The building with the steps on the right is the old Smithfield Street post office. Kaufmann's is two blocks further down.

When General Forbes took Fort Duquesne, he named the area between the three rivers "Pittsbourgh." Although the "o" was dropped in future references, the "h" remained. When Pittsburgh incorporated in 1816, the printer of the official documents accidentally left off the "h." The original charter for the Borough of Pittsburgh had the "h," but this document and many others were burned in the 1882 County Court House fire. At about the time the charter with the "h" was burning, the United States Board of Geographic Names recommended that all place names ending with the "berg" sound be spelled "burg" and cited Pittsburgh's 1816 incorporation papers (with the printer's error) for documentation. President Benjamin Harrison approved the Board's recommendations, and in 1891, Pittsburgh officially lost its "h." Many Pittsburghers objected strenuously; existing documents proved the validity of the "h." After a number of petitions and the help of influential State Senator George T. Oliver, the Geographic Board reconsidered its position. In 1911, Pittsburgh became the only "burg" in the country with an "h" at the end. Postcards printed before 1911, like this one, feature the "h"-less spelling.

During the construction of his medieval-Romanesque masterpiece, architect Henry Hobson Richardson was reported to have said, "If they honor me for the pygmy things I've done, what will they say when they see the Pittsburgh Court House." Richardson's courthouse was practical and beautiful. The stone and exterior detailing were designed to circumvent the soot in Pittsburgh's air. The great tower theoretically worked as a fresh air intake mechanism that drew in air "beyond the smoke strata" and circulated it throughout the building. Most importantly, since Pittsburgh's two previous courthouses had burned down, Richardson designed his courthouse to be fireproof. Unfortunately, he died of Bright's disease two years before the courthouse was

Allegheny County Court House, Pittsburgh, Pa.

completed. Inside the Court House, an inscription etched on the blocks at the entrance to the Law Library reads: "In Memory of Henry Hobson Richardson, Architect, 1838-1886 — Genius and training made him master of his profession. Although he died in the prime of life, he left to his country many monuments of art, foremost among them this temple of Justice."

The building has been only slightly modified over the years and is generally regarded as Pittsburgh's greatest architectural treasure.

Bridge of Sighs, from Court House to County Jail, Pittsburg, Pa.

The Bridge of Sighs leads from this jail complex to the County Courthouse, out of view to the left. In 1902, Warden Peter Soffel lived in the windowed structure when his wife, Catherine, became the most notorious criminal ever to occupy this building. In 1901, Ed and John Biddle were condemned to hang for the murders of a county detective and a Mount Washington grocer. The younger brother, Ed, twenty-four years old, was so handsome and charismatic that women packed the courthouse during his trial to get a look at him. Mrs. Soffel visited the brothers during their incarceration at the jail and provided them with saws. While the brothers worked on the bars, Mrs. Soffel read to them from the Bible loudly enough to mask the noise. In January, 1902, the brothers escaped from Richardson's jail with a gun provided by Mrs. Soffel; she escaped with them from her boring marriage. During an intense police chase, they were gunned down near Butler County. The Biddle boys died of their wounds. Mrs. Soffel, shot once, survived to experience life from the inside of a jail cell. In a Hollywood recreation of this story, Diane Keaton played a young Mrs. Soffel, inexperienced in the ways of the world. During the trial, however, Mrs. Soffel's maid suggested that Ed Biddle was just the tragic end in a string of dangerous liaisons.

Evelyn Nesbit was one of the great beauties of her age. As a New York chorus girl, she sipped sparkling wine with a number of prominent and wealthy men, including famous architect Stanford White. In 1905, she married Harry K. Thaw, son of the wealthy Pittsburgh industrialist William Thaw. Harry became convinced that White was plotting to take Evelyn away from him. In June, 1906, Harry and Evelyn attended an opening night performance of a play in Madison Square Garden. Stanford White was also in attendance. Harry Thaw shot Stanford White in the head.

The Thaw trial was even more sensational than the Soffel trial. Harry's mother paid Evelyn quite a sum of money—rumored to be $200,000—to take the stand and declare her husband an angel and a saint. The first jury could not reach a verdict; a second pronounced him not guilty by reason of insanity. He was sentenced to a mental institution. The Thaws divorced during Harry's institutionalization. Here, in a postcard copyrighted in 1907, Evelyn poses with her cat.

DIAMOND BANK BLDG., PITTSBURG, PA.   1054

The Diamond National Bank opened for business in 1870 on a location bordering Diamond Square (now Market Square) to serve the farmers, hucksters, and other lower-income working people who brought their goods to the markets at the Square. The Diamond Bank relocated to Fifth and Liberty around 1875 when they received their national charter. The building shown here, also at Fifth and Liberty, was built around 1905. A run on deposit withdrawals during the Depression forced the bank to close in the 1930's. A new bank, the Pitt National Bank, chartered in 1933, assumed responsibility for Diamond Bank deposits that had been frozen. Pitt merged with the Farmers Bank in the late 1940's and became part of the Mellon Banking empire. This building still stands; a Mellon Bank branch is located on the first floor.

In the 18th and early 19th centuries, Philadelphia was the nation's leading mercantile trade center. When New York's Erie Canal shifted the balance of trade to rival New York City in 1825, Pennsylvania attempted to direct trade back to Philadelphia with a canal system of its own from Philadelphia to Pittsburgh, constructed across Pennsylvania's variegated, mountainous terrain. But travel on it was slow and tedious, even dangerous. In the winter, the canals froze over. When steam-powered locomotives came into use in the 1830's, the canal system was ditched in favor of a rail line. The Pennsylvania Railroad was given the opportunity to create this line—provided it could raise sufficient capital and build a stipulated amount of roadbed within a fixed period of time. If not, then the rail rights would go to the already established B & O Railroad. The upstart P. R. R. met the state's stipulations handily, putting the powerful B & O out of the picture. The P. R. R. built itself into one of the largest railroads in the world by keeping other major lines out of Pennsylvania.

The balance of trade never shifted back to Phila-delphia, but Pennsylvania did have a great railroad. The structure seen here, with its distinctive domed rotunda, was designed by D. H. Burnham. It was the fourth Union Station.

8162   UNION STATION, PITTSBURGH, PA.

B. & O. Station, Pittsburg, Pa.

For years, the Baltimore and Ohio Railroad tried to bring a line into Pittsburgh. They were frustrated time and again by the mighty Pennsylvania Railroad, but finally opened a line here in 1871. Even so, they did not have a proper Pittsburgh depot until the late 1880's. The Queen Anne-style station pictured here, designed by noted architect Frank Furness, was built along the Mon near the Smithfield Street Bridge between 1880-1890. It functioned as a rail station into the 1950's when it was demolished as part of the Penn-Lincoln parkway project.

Wabash Passenger Depot, Liberty and Ferry Sts., Pittsburg, Pa.

Railroad baron Jay Gould dreamed of creating a rail line from San Francisco to New York. Pittsburgh, with its tremendous volume of industrial freight, was a big part of Gould's dream. Andrew Carnegie, who complained relentlessly about being overcharged by the Pennsylvania Railroad, promised Gould freight business for his new line, although this was probably a ploy on Carnegie's part to get the P. R. R. to lower its rates for him. Gould took Carnegie at his word, fought the P. R. R., endured hardships and setbacks that damaged his physical health, and spent a tremendous amount of money— putting at stake the assets of his Western lines—to drive a line of rails over the western end of the Mon into downtown Pittsburgh. Gould opened the magnificent Beaux-Arts terminal pictured in this postcard in 1904. Unfortunately, by the time the Wabash-Pittsburgh was completed, Carnegie had sold his steel interests to J. P. Morgan. "Gould's Folly" went into receivership four years later in 1908. The Wabash Station was used as office space through most of its existence. It was demolished in 1955.

The Pittsburgh and Lake Erie Railroad, chartered in 1873, originally ran from Pittsburgh to Connellsville, carrying coal, coke and passengers from western Pennsylvania to the Lake Erie region. Cornelius Vanderbilt and his New York Central, arch rivals of the Pennsylvania Railroad, bought stock in the P&LE, thus gaining a foothold in the Pittsburgh area. The original station, a small one located at West Carson and Smithfield, proved inadequate to handle the increased freight requirements of the late 19th century business boom. Construction on the new Terminal Building,

523   P. & L. E R. R DEPOT, PITTSBURGH PA.   ILLUSTRATED POST CARD CO., N. Y.

pictured here, began in 1899. The exterior of the building is of a classical design with some Beaux-Arts detailing. The interior's lavishly colored, neo-Baroque design, crowned with a magnificent, stained glass, vaulted ceiling, makes it one of Pittsburgh's most beautiful interior spaces. When rail traffic declined after World War II, the Terminal Building's grand waiting room went largely unused. With the financial backing of several of Pittsburgh's most prominent citizens, the Pittsburgh History and Landmarks Foundation developed the P&LE property into Station Square, a waterfront complex of offices, restaurants, upscale shopping, entertainment facilities, and a hotel. The waiting room has been restored and adapted as a restaurant.

The first Smithfield Street Bridge, a wooden covered bridge, was built in 1818 and was used primarily to cart coal from Coal Hill (Mount Washington) into town. This bridge burned, along with much of Pittsburgh, in the great fire of 1845. The next bridge

was designed by John Roebling, champion of the suspension bridge. The bridge in this card is the third and current Smithfield Street Bridge. Its elongated figure-eight trusses represent an unusual stress distribution system known as "lenticulation." Designed by Gustave Lindenthal and built 1881-1883, the Smithfield is one of the last lenticular bridges in the United States.

SMITHFIELD STREET BRIDGE, PITTSBURGH, PA.   8060

When Pittsburgh needed more space, it expanded north first, then east. But the mountainous terrain between The Golden Triangle and the south hills posed a serious problem. Inclines were an awkward form of transportation at best, particularly in the automobile age. It was landscape architect Frederick Law Olmsted who first suggested boring tunnels into the hillside. The Liberty Tunnels, or Liberty Tubes as they are known, opened in 1928.

At one time, Carson Street on the South Side was part of a small city known as Birmingham. Carson Street was its Main Street. Notice the old streetcar with the cow catcher.

The South Side has preserved many of its Victorian buildings, although store fronts have been modernized. It has become trendy in recent years and is sometimes called Pittsburgh's Soho.

KAUFMANN'S, THE BIG STORE, PITTSBURGH, PA.

In 1871, Jacob and Isaac Kaufmann, Jewish-German immigrants, opened a small tailoring business in Birmingham (now the South Side). A third brother, Morris, came over from Germany to help out, followed by a fourth brother, Henry. Although they sold mostly clothing, the inventory included other dry goods. The business expanded and relocated three times before moving into a four-story building on the corner of Smithfield Street and Diamond Alley (now Forbes Avenue) in 1877.

In this postcard, the first Smithfield Street building is on the right, although the building had been considerably altered by this time. At a later date, an addition was added to the top of this structure. The Kaufmann brothers used fair practice, good prices, a wide variety of quality products, and innovative advertising to get the jump on their competition. The store stretched the length of an entire city block by 1885 when it came to be known as "The Big Store." Kaufmann's, now owned by the May Company, is still open for business at this downtown location.

KAUFMAN & BAER CO.,
Department Store,
Pittsburgh, Pa.

As the original Kaufmann's Department Store expanded, the Kaufmann brothers brought in cousins from Germany to assist in the store's development. These cousins shared in the profits but were not made partners. At one point, the cousins attempted to take over the management of the store — a retail coup d'etat. The Kaufmann brothers staged a re-organization move that resulted in incorporation with Edgar J. Kaufmann, son of Morris Kaufmann, as head of the organization. The cousins were installed somewhere outside of the organization. They decided to open a rival store — Kaufmann & Baer — down the street. For a time they were successful; but ultimately, they lacked the retail savvy of the Kaufmann brothers and sold out to Gimbel Brothers in the 1920's.

Pittsburgh is a city of wide ethnic diversity. The Germania Bank served the many German people who settled in this area; bank employees could speak both German and English.

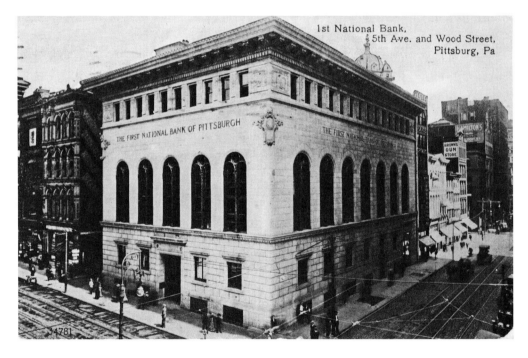

The First National Bank was established in 1852 as the Pittsburgh Trust and Savings Co. It was the first bank in Pittsburgh to receive a national charter (1863). This building opened at the corner of Fifth Avenue and Wood Street in 1909. The design, by D. H. Burnham and Co., was inspired by a palace in Sienna, Italy, belonging to the Piccolomini family. The First National Bank anticipated building vertically sometime in the future, so this building had a deep, massive foundation and a steel frame strong enough to allow up to twenty-two stories to be added—which happened less than four years later. Since the building only looked like this for about four years, this card is relatively rare.

The First National Bank evolved into the Pittsburgh National Bank. PNB razed this structure to make way for a modern building.

FARMERS BANK BUILDING   PITTSBURG, PA
At Fifth Avenue and Wood Street. The highest and most imposing structure in Pittsburg. It towers Twenty-four stories above the street

A Farmers Bank publication cites the bank's establishment in 1832, although a charter for a Farmers and Mechanics Bank dates to 1816. This bank served primarily lower-income working people.

The early Pittsburgh skyscraper featured on this postcard opened at the corner of Fifth and Wood in 1903. A series of sculptures is spaced between the windows at the fourth floor level. These Grecian female figures represent banking interests and virtues such as Agriculture, Mechanics, Railroading, Courage, Wisdom and (right around the corner) Prosperity—the source of a few jokes during the Depression. At one time, a bust of a white bull terrier was located above the bank's entrance. This was "Prince," the bank's mascot, whose master was the bank's cashier. During the late 1800's, Prince was a favorite with bank customers, frequently keeping their children occupied while they transacted business. Prince disappeared shortly after a regiment of soldiers, en route to the Spanish American War, passed through town. The bank adopted Prince as their official logo.

The Farmers Bank became part of the Mellon banking empire during the second half of this century. This lovely building still

stands but has been covered with a brown metal sheath.

Westinghouse Building, Penn Ave., and 9th St., Pittsburg, Pa.

This was the first office building built with the Westinghouse name on it. It was erected in 1888-1889 and constructed completely of masonry. Around the turn of the century, this nine-story structure was expanded to twelve stories with steel beams added for reinforcement. It is said that George Westinghouse had this building erected at the corner of Penn and Ninth so that he could look out on the Pennsylvania Railroad where he had first demonstrated his air brake system. In this building, he sat at an 18-foot desk and administered such Westinghouse concerns as Philadelphia Company (natural gas), Westinghouse Air Brake Co., Westinghouse Electric and Manufacturing Co., and Union Switch & Signal Co. This building was demolished in 1941. However, that eighteen-foot desk, which was donated to the Chamber of Commerce, couldn't fit through any door, window, or staircase in the building. How did Westinghouse get it into his office?

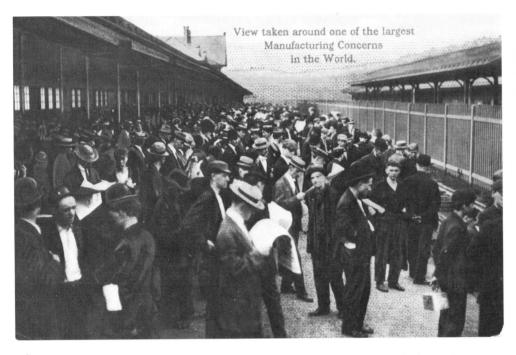

View taken around one of the largest Manufacturing Concerns in the World.

George Westinghouse built his fortune from the invention of the air brake, which used compressed air to apply braking pressure throughout a train of railcars. This greatly diminished the hazards of braking a train, and allowed trains to carry more cars and heavier loads.

In the late 1800's, Westinghouse realized that alternating current would be a cheaper, more efficient way to deliver electricity. But Thomas Edison advocated the direct current system. Westinghouse dramatically underbid Edison for the right to provide electrical power to the Chicago World's Fair of 1893. This turned out to be something of a PR coup. Westinghouse lost money on the World's Fair, but gained national acceptance for his electrical system.

As his Westinghouse Electric and Manufacturing Company expanded, Westinghouse relocated to the Turtle Creek area along a route established by the Pennsylvania Railroad. Turtle Creek became a burgeoning town. Here are Westinghouse Electric employees waiting at the Pennsylvania Station for the commuter train home.

This particular card is a colorized version of a photograph taken at Westinghouse Electric around 1905. At that time there were more women working in the electrical manufacturing companies than in any other field of manufacturing because the work was often tedious, requiring dexterity and patience. Here, the women are winding wire, paper, and tape around metal tubes for the

Street Car Armature Winding, Section S., Westinghouse Electric and M'f'g. Co., East Pittsburgh, Pa.

coils that created magnetic fields necessary for the electric motors to operate. These motors would run traction machines (streetcars). Armature winding was difficult work and took years to master. Women who did this work reported that their whole body shook during the process of working on these coils. Although this work paid more than work in a laundry or waiting on tables, the lowest paid man at Westinghouse Electric made more than the highest paid woman.

James O'Hara and Isaac Craig created Pittsburgh's first glassworks on the south side of the Monongahela River in 1795. Glass became the number one industry in Pittsburgh, but was soon demoted to second and, later, third place by the iron and steel industries. Collectors favor glass made by the Bakewell Glass House, which began operations in 1807. Bakewell plates were used at the White House in James Madison's time. By 1870, 68 glass factories in Pittsburgh were producing half of the glass made in the United States.

No child labor laws were in force early in this century; two of the workers in this photo look to be less than eighteen years old; the boy sitting down is probably less than twelve years. If anyone would hire you, you were old enough to work.

Pittsburg, Pa., Blowing Bottles in Glass Factory.

In the early 1800's, iron production plants were scattered at various locations throughout the United States. Advances in production techniques favored the use of coke, a product of bituminous coal found abundantly in and around the Pittsburgh area. This discovery transformed Pittsburgh from one of many manufacturing areas into a powerful industrial center. Most of the great Pittsburgh money was dug out of the ground by coal miners like the men pictured in this postcard.

The Coal Industry   Pittsburg, Pa.

In 1853 Benjamin Jones, Bernard Lauth, and John Lauth established iron puddling furnaces and rolling mills on the south bank of the Mon. Not long after that, James A. Laughlin built two powerful blast furnaces across the river on the north bank. The two companies worked in tandem for many years and eventually merged. In time Jones and Laughlin became a major producer of Bessemer steel, second only to the Carnegie steel works. Pittsburgh iron and steel companies liked to name their blast furnaces after the wives or daughters of investors and business partners. The Lucy furnaces of the Carnegie concerns, for instance, were named after the wife of Tom Carnegie. It is thought that Jones and Laughlin might have started this tradition with their Eliza furnaces. J & L ceased milling operations in 1979. Theirs had been the last plant left within Pittsburgh's city limits.

Scenes in Jones and Laughlin Steel Plant,
S. S. Pittsburgh, Pa.

Front View of Ladle Emptying Molten Metal into Moulds,
Pig Iron Machine. Pittsburg, Pa.

Copyright.

Metalworks was the backbone of an economy that transformed Pittsburgh from a backwoods frontier town into the third largest corporate headquarters in the United States. When plants in this area started to close, Pittsburghers decided that high-end technology would build their future. The stretch of land where the great Eliza blast furnaces once stood is now being transformed into a campus for high technology concerns.

This card shows a scene from a Pittsburgh metalworks plant, most likely J & L.

When Andrew Carnegie wanted to build his first steel mill, he knew he would need the good will of the Pennsylvania Railroad and the influence of its president, J. Edgar Thompson. He named his new works in Braddock The Edgar Thompson Works. Thompson did not have to invest in the works, nor did he receive an iota of interest, but Carnegie successfully drew upon Thompson's pride of parenthood many times. The E. T. Works received its first order for 2000 steel rails in 1875 from (who else?) The Pennsylvania Railroad.

This mill was built on Braddock's Field, the site of the historic battle between English General Edward Braddock, and French and Indian forces.

Railroad expansion peaked toward the last quarter of the nineteenth century, lessening the demand for steel rails that had nurtured the great Pittsburgh steel industry. Andrew Carnegie's Edgar Thompson works expanded into the "merchant steel" market, producing steel ingots for the manufacturers of everyday steel products such as nails, stove pipes, buggy springs, etc. A group of these manufacturers decided to cut costs by producing their own steel ingots. They formed a syndicate, Pittsburgh Bessemer Steel Company, in 1879 and built this mill along the river's edge in the developing community of Homestead. Andrew Kloman, an embittered ex-business partner of Andrew Carnegie, invested his money and engineering genius in the new enterprise, determined to put Carnegie out of business. In its first year, Pittsburgh Bessemer stole 20% of Carnegie's merchant steel market. Shortly thereafter, however, an economic depression, coupled with serious labor problems at the unionized Homestead works, created serious financial problems for the fledgling mill. Bessemer's partners, excepting Kloman, approached Andrew Carnegie with a buy-out offer; within three years of operation, the Homestead works became part of the Carnegie steel empire.

Although Andrew Carnegie was born into a family of active trade unionists and championed the rights of working men through union membership and participation, his maniacal obsession with keeping costs down put him at odds with the unions in his own mills. In 1892, Carnegie conspired with his manager, Henry Clay Frick, to run the unions out of the labor-plagued Homestead works. That summer, while Carnegie was abroad in Scotland, Frick posted notices in the plant that Carnegie Steel was converting to a non-union shop and would no longer negotiate with the Amalgamated Association of Iron and Steel Workers. Union and non-union workers promptly walked out—precisely what Frick wanted. He locked them out, erected a barbed-wire plank fence around the plant (complete with rifle holes), and secretly contracted the services of 300 armed men from the Pinkerton Detective Agency to protect the strike breakers he intended to bring in. The striking men expected these actions from Frick: scouts watched the riverways and rail lines day and night. Early on July 6, a steamer towing two barges of Pinkerton agents was spotted passing under the Smithfield Street Bridge. By the time Frick's Pinkerton agents reached the Homestead plant, most of the town was waiting at the river's edge. In an all-day battle, Homesteaders fired at the agents with guns, rifles, and small cannon. Oil was poured into the river and ignited. At 4 p.m., the Pinkerton agents agreed to surrender their arms and leave the area immediately, never to return, in exchange for a safe docking. But when the 300 agents, dressed in the new Pinkerton uniforms hated by working men, began to file on shore, they were beaten, stripped of their clothes, and maimed with rocks and pieces of iron. Three men were killed and virtually every Pinkerton agent suffered an injury. Despite a national scandal and near universal support for Homestead's working men, Carnegie and Frick managed to oust the union. The Carnegie concerns remained non-union as long as Carnegie owned them.

"JOE MAGARAC" BY WILLIAM GROPPER
ONE OF 116 PAINTINGS WHICH REPRESENT A
"PORTRAIT OF PENNSYLVANIA"
KNOWN AS THE GIMBEL PENNSYLVANIA ART COLLECTION

The original of this picture of Joe Magarac, painted by Western Pennsylvania artist William Gropper, was part of an exhibit sponsored in 1946 by Gimbels Department Store. Joe is a folk hero known to old-time iron and steel workers. Born in a mountain of ore, Joe is the worker's worker—able to stir a cauldron of molten metal with his fingers and shape hot steel rails with his bare hands. Whenever a tragic accident is about to occur, Joe appears out of nowhere to save endangered metalworkers. Another side to the legend, however, says that Magarac means "jackass" in Croatian. In one story, Joe enters a competition to win the hand of the beautiful daughter of a local farmer. Joe wins with a spectacular flourish but declines the hand of the girl because marriage would interfere with his work in the mills. Thus, Joe is a double-edged mythological figure: a hero for his superior strength and commitment to his fellow metalworkers, and a jackass for being a beast of burden with no thought for his own pleasure.

Fort Pitt Hotel, Pittsburg, Pa.

In the early 1900's, there were several first-class hotels in the downtown area: the Monongahela House, the William Penn, and this one, the Fort Pitt. Built in 1905, the Fort Pitt Hotel was located at Penn and Tenth across from Pennsylvania Station. Both the Monongahela House and the Fort Pitt suffered when the primary mode of transportation shifted from boats and trains to automobiles and airplanes. The Fort Pitt is gone now.

THE ENGLISH ROOM, FORT PITT HOTEL, PITTSBURGH, PA.

Sumptuous, comfortable, manly in an Edwardian way—that was the Fort Pitt Hotel. Most visitors in the age of industry were men, so Pittsburgh hotels featured a rugged style of interior decoration. Wood paneling around the room was dark and elaborately carved. One wall carving featured a re-creation of the official seal of the City of Pittsburgh.

The Norse Room in the manliest of Pittsburgh's hotels had a vaulted ceiling of Rookwood tiles, walls covered with bas-relief dramatizations of Viking epics, massive columns decorated with gargoyles, and large replicas of Viking ships done in brass and copper hanging from the ceiling. One wall panel illustrated Longfellow's poem "The Skeleton in Armor." The Norse Room was a cafe located in the basement of the hotel. Unfortunately, when the Fort Pitt was demolished, not much could be saved from this room, as the whole thing was anchored in concrete. There are some reports that this room actually lies semi-intact somewhere below the Vista Hotel.

William Penn Hotel, Pittsburgh, Pa.

The William Penn Hotel, built in 1916 by Janssen & Abbott, is the last of the great hotels from the early 20th century to still serve the public. From its inception, it was meant to be The Golden Triangle's most elegant hotel. In the 1920's, theatrical designer Joseph Urban, who had created Art Deco stage designs for the Ziegfeld Follies, designed a magnificent meeting room/ballroom for the hotel. The Urban Room is one of the few Art Deco interiors left in the city.

Pittsburgh's downtown area, sandwiched between two large rivers, is prone to floods. This advertising card from the Hotel Antler lists a few of the more damaging floods in Pittsburgh history. Most flood cards show scenes from the one in 1907, which reached a record level of 36+ feet.

FEDERAL STREET ALLEGHENY DURING THE FLOOD

Nowadays, newscasters advise people to stay indoors at the first drop of a snowflake. During the flood of 1907, Pittsburghers were expected to continue—this was a working town, and there was work to be done. Here is a wagon train making its way along lower Federal Street en route to town via the Sixth Street Bridge.

No. 11.   Federal Street, Allegheny.

Even with floodwaters receding a bit, canoes were needed to carry bowler-hatted men in business suits to various destinations. After every devastating flood, a dam system to control the waters was talked about until financing came up. On St. Patrick's Day, 1936, the worst flood in Pittsburgh history occurred. The water level exceeded 46 feet, more than 135,000 people were made homeless, valuable historic documents stored downtown were destroyed, and property damage exceeded $200,000,000. After this event, the city came up with flood control money; no serious flooding problem has occurred in The Golden Triangle since 1936.

LIBERTY AVENUE AND MARKET STREET, PITTSBURGH, PA.

Liberty Avenue, downtown Pittsburgh's Main Street, is in the foreground of this scene. Market Street veers up to the left and leads to the historic Market Square area. The little wedge of buildings in the center still stands, although in a somewhat altered form. Down Liberty Avenue are the Diamond Bank and the Wabash Station.

Fifth Avenue, East from Wood Street, Pittsburgh, Pa.

This is Fifth Avenue looking east, circa 1912. Woolworth's is still with us as this book goes to press, although it looks different. The Grand Theater can be seen four doors down. In the extreme left foreground is the entrance to the Farmer's National Bank; note the bank's mascot, Prince, over the entrance.

Fifth Avenue, Pittsburgh, Pa.
1758————Sesqui-Centennial————1908

The Sesqui-centennial of 1908 celebrated the 150th anniversary of General John Forbes taking of Fort Duquesne on November 25, 1758. Forbes named the area "Pittsbourgh" in a letter penned that day to England's Prime Minister, William Pitt. The Sesqui-centennial may have been the grandest pageant ever staged in Pittsburgh. Signs identifying historic sites were placed throughout the city. Merchants created window displays illustrating historic events that occurred near their businesses. City office buildings decorated their facades with elaborate lighting configurations and flags. The city's Decoration Committee produced a razzle-dazzle walkway of ornamental pillars called "The Court of Honor" that began under an elaborate arch at Grant Street and Fifth Avenue, and culminated under an arch on Liberty Avenue. This card shows the path of the Court of Honor.

The Sesqui-centennial's events commenced on Sunday, September 27, when all of the churches in the city simultaneously rang their bells. The city sponsored special events throughout the following week. One afternoon, an aeronautics display, featuring a Zeppelin, was held in Schenley Park. At the Western Exhibition's Music Hall, a concert of music composed by Pittsburghers was held. On Wednesday, a River Parade on the Mon illustrated the evolution of river traffic, opening with a fleet of Indian canoes; then came rough timber rafts, flat boats, keel boats, and eventually fifty large steamboats led by a replica of *The New Orleans,* reportedly the first steamboat to travel on these waters. Even more spectacular was the street parade that closed the Sesqui-centennial celebration. Industries, businesses, organizations, fraternities, unions, regiments, and special interest groups participated. The float sponsored by the Boggs & Buhl Department Store was pulled by 46 horses while the Heinz float was pulled by 15 teams of 30 horses.

111:—New Mellon National Bank Bldg., Pittsburgh, Pa.

Thomas Mellon (1813-1908) established a successful law practice after graduating from Western University. In 1859, he was elected judge of common pleas court of Allegheny County. Upon retiring, he established a bank on Smithfield Street near where the Oliver Building stands today. In 1873, T. Mellon & Sons (Andrew and Richard) moved to 514 Smithfield Street; Judge Mellon had already made a $10,000 loan to Henry Clay Frick that resulted in the Frick Coke Co. With an uncanny degree of insight, the Mellon brothers managed to invest in coke, iron, steel, transportation, oil, and aluminum just before each exploded into multi-million dollar concerns. Alcoa, Koppers, and Gulf Oil were built with Mellon money—this family bankrolled Pittsburgh's evolution into a world-class capital of manufacturing.

In 1902, T. Mellon & Sons incorporated as the Mellon National Bank. Between 1923-1924, the bank building pictured on this linen card was erected between Oliver and Fifth. Although banks all over town were erecting skyscrapers, the most powerful bank chose to build a four-story structure.

Dollar Savings Bank,
Pittsburgh, Pa.

By the 1870's there were nearly ninety banking institutions within Pittsburgh and Allegheny City. The Dollar Savings Bank, shown in this postcard, was incorporated in 1855 as Pittsburgh's first foray into mutual banking, where the institution functions for the benefit of its depositors, rather than for investors. This brownstone building was erected on Fourth Street between 1869-1871. The bank, this building, and those lions posted at the entrance still exist today.

THE BANK OF PITTSBURG, PA.   1055

The Bank of Pittsburgh was the first bank in this area chartered with local money. Known in 1810 as the Pittsburgh Manufacturing Company, it reorganized as the Bank of Pittsburgh in 1814. This Roman temple of finance was built on Fourth Street, the street of banks, in 1895. Its design was inspired by the neo-classicism of the 1893 Chicago World's Fair. The Bank of Pittsburgh closed its doors in the early years of the Depression. According to architectural historian James D. Van Trump, local architect Edward W. Griffith wanted the bank's pillars but didn't have a specific use for them in mind. The building proper was demolished in the 1940's, but the facade stood for several years until Griffith could take the pillars away. For a few years, downtown Pittsburgh had its own Roman ruins.

In the latter half of the 19th century, oil from Titusville came down the Allegheny River to the Port of Pittsburgh to be sold to oil traders, who bid for the oil there at the wharves. They eventually organized The Pittsburgh Brokers Association, which evolved into The Pittsburgh Oil Exchange. As the importance of oil in this area diminished and that of industrial stocks increased, the name was changed to The Pittsburgh Stock & Oil Exchange. In 1896, "oil" was removed altogether. The national prominence of Pittsburgh industries made this stock exchange a lively enterprise. In this century, however, Pittsburgh concerns came to be traded on the New York Stock Exchange. The Pittsburgh exchange closed its doors in 1974.

This is the Pittsburgh Stock Exchange building, originally located at 229-233 Fourth Avenue.

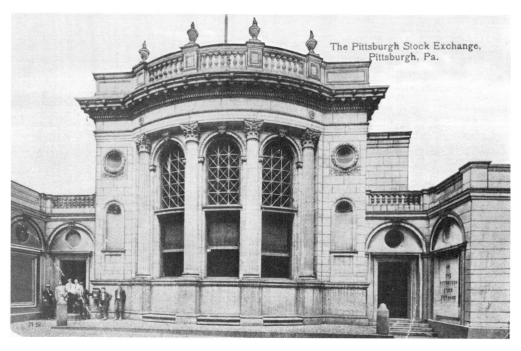

The Pittsburgh Stock Exchange,
Pittsburgh, Pa.

Because of the Stock Exchange and the large number of banks along this street, Fourth Avenue became known as "The Wall Street of Pittsburgh." Although the exchange is gone, much of old "Wall Street" still looks as it did in the first decade of this century. Preservationists and concerned citizens have petitioned the city to have the area officially designated an historic district.

A view of The Point from the West End. The covered wooden bridge leading from Allegheny City (the North Side) to The Point had been removed; the Manchester Bridge had not yet been built. Note the river front space along both banks of the Ohio. Pittsburgh, its rivers, and its land existed for one purpose only: work.

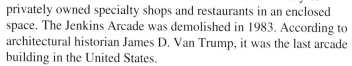

Jenkins' Arcade Building,
Fifth, Liberty and Penn Aves.,
Pittsburg, Pa.

This building's predecessor was a six-story warehouse built by Thomas C. Jenkins around 1864. It stored and sold roast coffees, teas, flour, tobacco, and a variety of dry goods. In those days, the Pennsylvania Railroad had tracks running down Liberty Avenue to the Mon Wharf with a special spur for Jenkins' warehouse that enabled railcars to enter his building and unload. This popular Pittsburgh spot burned down in 1897. In 1911, Thomas Jenkins' heirs built a large shop and office complex on this site in the then-popular arcade style. It was the first shopping center in Pittsburgh to offer a wide variety of privately owned specialty shops and restaurants in an enclosed space. The Jenkins Arcade was demolished in 1983. According to architectural historian James D. Van Trump, it was the last arcade building in the United States.

Interior Jenkins Arcade, Pittsburg, Pa.

This is an artist's rendering of the stately marble and brass interior of the Jenkins Arcade in the early 1900's. It was estimated that 36,000 people strolled through it each day, shopping for clothes, candy, gifts, office supplies, books, and furniture. In the offices upstairs, the services of doctors, dentists, optometrists, tutors, music teachers, and dance instructors were available. Tea rooms were in vogue, and the Jenkins Arcade had a Japanese tea room called The Sacred Urn.

SIXTH AVE. AND DUQUESNE CLUB, PITTSBURG, PA.   1061

The Duquesne Club was created in 1873 along the lines of the traditional English men's club, except that membership had more to do with business acumen than noble lineage. A third of the original members were from the iron and steel industry; the other two-thirds included executives of the glass industry, bankers, physicians, lawyers, and retailers. When some of the club's younger members splintered off to form the Pittsburgh Club, Duquesne Club members moved from Penn Avenue to new diggings uptown. The new clubhouse built by Longfellow, Alden and Harlow opened at 325 Sixth Avenue in 1890. Despite a clubhouse rule against doing business on the premises, the facilities functioned as the ultimate boardroom where notes were compared, informal agreements reached, and the direction of Pittsburgh commerce decided.

The center building with bay windows and awnings on the right of the street is the Duquesne Club.

During the mid-to-late 1880's, lower Penn Avenue, the district near Hornes, was posh and ritzy—the Park Avenue of Pittsburgh. Many beautiful homes were built there, including this one, the home of millionaire industrialist John H. Schoenberger. In 1873 this became the first home of the exclusive Duquesne Club.

A rift in the Duquesne Club's membership occurred about six years after it was formed when some younger members thought some older members were too stuffy. This rebellious crew seceded and formed the Pittsburgh Club. They bought the Schoenberger mansion in 1884; it was the official clubhouse until 1942 when dwindling membership and mounting debt forced them to sell the property. The club moved into a suite in the William Penn Hotel. This building was later demolished to make way for the Gateway Towers development.

PITTSBURG, PA. Pittsburg Club, Penn. Ave.

1320

TRINITY CHURCH, PITTSBURG.

Trinity is one of the oldest churches in the city, representing a congregation that dates back to 1787. Pictured here is the third and current Trinity Church, built in 1872. It was built upon the site of Pittsburgh's oldest burial grounds. According to reports, this location once held an Indian burial mound seven stories high. The French at Fort Duquesne also buried their dead on this land. A portion of this 400-year-old graveyard still exists — the oldest landmark in the Golden Triangle. There were originally more than 4,000 graves on this site. Among the 128 still buried here are Christopher Cowan, the man who established the first rolling mill in the area; William Eichbaum, founder of the first glass-cutting factory in Pittsburgh; and Red Pole, a Village Chief of the Shawnee.

The McCreery Department Store in the McCreery Building opened around 1904 under the direction of Manhattan merchant John Claflin. It catered to the carriage trade—members of Pittsburgh's newly monied elite, who usually preferred to shop in New York City. For many years, McCreery's elegant dining room was Pittsburgh's most popular meet-and-eat spot. The store fell from grace with the public in the late 1920's when Parrot Fever broke out in the pet shop—dangerous for humans as well as birds. Eight McCreery's employees died from it. During the next decade, the interior was renovated, a new manager brought in, and a unique line of merchandise put out; but it was all in vain. McCreery's closed its doors in 1938, although the building still stands.

MC CREERY DINING ROOM, PITTSBURG, PA.

Here is McCreery's famous dining room with its warm, richly furnished interior; linen tablecloths and napkins; fine china and silver service—common before World War II. After the war, everyday standards fell, and these kind of amenities could only be found in country club dining rooms and restaurants catering to a monied clientele. In the last decade, a restaurant renaissance in Pittsburgh has harkened the return of an updated version of the simple elegance that Edwardian Pittsburghers took for granted.

STEAM SHOVEL IN ACTION REMOVING THE HUMP, PITTSBURGH, PA.

Pittsburgh's steep hillsides, cliffs, and ravines created many engineering challenges. The area from The Point up to Smithfield Street was relatively flat. Then a rise up to Grant's Hill was so steep—over sixty feet in some places—that horse-drawn vehicles had great difficulty making the climb. Their drivers dubbed this area "the hump." The city first cut into the hump in 1836 and again in 1847. This second cut left St. Paul's Church over fifteen feet above street level—"a regular castle in the air," as one Pittsburgher described it. Steep wooden steps had to be built up to the doors. The church burned down in 1851 because fire crews could not get into it to put out the fire. The final cut in the hump, shown here in progress, commenced in 1912 and took eighteen months to complete. This is Fifth Avenue looking into town. The Richardson Courthouse is on the left.

Carnegie Building,
Pittsburgh, Pa.

Lucy Carnegie, for whom the famous Lucy Furnace was named, erected this building in honor of her husband, Thomas, who died in his early forties. He was the younger brother of Andrew. In 1893, construction began on this steel-framed skyscraper, the first in Pittsburgh and one of the first in the world. Carnegie Steel's structural engineer, F. H. Kindl, took charge of the project. The frame stood for a year to demonstrate dramatically the strength and durability of steel, which allowed buildings to withstand high wind pressure. This 13-story office building caused quite a sensation in Pittsburgh, a town where most buildings were two to four stories high. Office workers taking the fast, new elevators to the Carnegie Building's upper levels felt as if they were soaring into heaven. After this building was sold in 1951, it was demolished to clear the way for an addition to Kaufmann's Department Store.

Oliver Building, Pittsburg. Pa

Henry Oliver and Andrew Carnegie grew up together in old Allegheny. As young men, they ran messages for a Pittsburgh telegraph office. Unlike Carnegie, who built his fortune one calculated step at a time, Oliver was inclined to adventurous speculation, making and losing half a dozen fortunes. When high-grade Bessemer iron ore was discovered in the Mesabi Range in Minnesota, Oliver quickly winked his way into a partnership in an established Mesabi mining operation on money he didn't have. He offered Carnegie Steel a 50% partnership for a $500,000 loan. Although Carnegie mistrusted his old friend, he eventually relented. The Mesabi mining operation made millions of dollars for Oliver and Carnegie. Upon selling his mining and steel interests, Oliver invested in Pittsburgh real estate. He died in 1904. His estate erected this classically-styled office building in his honor between 1908-1910.

When Henry Clay Frick saw the success of the Jenkins Arcade he decided to build his own — but on a grander scale. Architect Frederick Osterling created the Gothic fantasy pictured on this postcard. When it opened in 1917, Frick's Union Arcade was the largest such facility in the world, featuring 240 retail shops between the first four floors and office space up to the twin towers on the roof. The twin towers have contributed quite a bit to the folklore of Pittsburgh. Frick purchased the land for his arcade from the Catholic Diocese. It was rumored that, to seal the deal, Frick promised to build a chapel in the new building. Many people still believe there is a chapel located inside one of these towers. Not so — both towers contain office suites. The Union Trust Company bought this building from the Frick estate in 1922. Although there are still a few shops on the ground floor, it has long since ceased to function as an arcade.

THE UNION TRUST CO. OF PITTSBURGH BLDG., PITTSBURGH, PA.

Architect Frederick J. Osterling designed this wedding-cake skyscraper built between 1901-1902 on the corner of Fourth Avenue and Wood Street. The interior has recently been renovated to suit contemporary office taste; otherwise, it has survived relatively unscathed into modern times. The tiny lobby of the Arrott Building is stunning—colorful, veined marble; gracefully powerful bronze; ornate ceramic accents; and a marble stairway.

Photo by Johnston

ARROTT BUILDING, PITTSBURGH

This card prominently features one of those grand, old, multiple-story Woolworth 5 & 10's. Note the candy-striped awnings over many of the windows. On the day this photograph was taken, a sale or demonstration was going on at Woolworth's.

Concentrated on this one little corner of Liberty Avenue are most of the forms of transportation available in this century's first decade: a horse-drawn cab (probably a commercial carrier or delivery vehicle), an early electrically-powered trolley with open windows (no glass), a Model-T automobile, and a larger trolley with adjustable glass windows.

This Woolworth's was torn down in the 1970's to make way for the Heinz Hall Plaza.

Here is the corner of Sixth and Liberty at street level, facing east up Liberty Avenue. The Woolworth store is located on the left. Across the street is a gently curving building still in existence today. When this photo was taken, the building housed the Rosenbaum Company's pharmacy. An advertising sign hanging vertically from this building indicates the offices of "Dentists."

Fifth Avenue East from
Liberty Avenue, Pittsburgh, Pa.

This is the corner of Fifth and Liberty, looking east up Fifth. Liberty Avenue is out of the picture to the left. The free-standing clock in front of the Diamond (now Mellon) Bank lasted into the 1960's when it was destroyed in a street accident.

Keenan Building,
Pittsburgh, Pa.

Colonel James J. Keenan founded *The Evening Penny Press* in 1884. Later, it became *The Pittsburgh Press* (one of two 19th-century Pittsburgh newspapers still publishing today). When Keenan retired from the newspaper business, he ventured into the real estate market. This 1907 building was patterned after a building he admired in San Francisco; its slender silhouette and graceful dome contrast sharply with the city's masculine-looking, block-long rectangles in the sky. A number of terra-cotta portraits of historical figures grace the sides of the building between the first and second floors: Mary Schenley, Andrew Carnegie, Stephen Collins Foster, William Pitt, and George Washington, among others. This once towering structure has been dwarfed by recent development in the area.

KOPPERS BUILDING, GULF BUILDING
FEDERAL RESERVE BANK
PITTSBURGH, PA. 21

Early skyscrapers, like the Oliver and Frick buildings, started at the edge of the sidewalk and went straight up into the air. This was fine when there were only one or two skyscrapers around. When there got to be a lot of them, they blocked out the sun. Architects solved this problem by creating buildings that stepped back as they got higher, usually tapering to a point. The "Moderne" style of these buildings is known as "Art Deco" today. The Koppers building (left) and the Gulf building (right) are two of Pittsburgh's finest Art Deco skyscrapers.

This 25-story hotel was built on Diamond Street (now Forbes Avenue) and Cherry Way in 1928 by Andrew and Richard Mellon for about $2,000,000. It had all the latest conveniences, including a shower in every bathroom and a tub in most of them. The hotel advertised that the air in each guest room changed every six minutes while the air in the dining room changed every 4.5 minutes. The Pittsburgher, located just a stone's throw away from the County Court House and the City County Building, was a favorite haunt of judges, lawyers, and political figures. Sports figures also liked the Pittsburgher's Travelers Bar. The hotel went out of business in 1965. The structure was converted for office use and is known today as the Lawyers Building.

THE PITTSBURGHER - PITTSBURGH, PA.

PUBLIC
AUDITORIUM PITTSBURGH, PA

Courtesy Wonday Film Service

The Civic Arena is an architectural and engineering marvel. Its stainless steel cantilevered dome is divided into eight leaves, two of which are stationary while the other six retract. It is 415 feet in diameter, 136 feet high, and retracts at the touch of a button in 2.5 minutes.

This monolithic urban entertainment center began with a rather modest concept. The Civic Light Opera needed a home. Councilman Abe Wolk thought it would be nice to build a little theater in the wooded surroundings of Highland Park. This theater would have a retractable roof so that on warm summer evenings theater goers could indulge in the subtle magic of an outdoor performance. Abe's charming idea took on monstrous proportions as it worked its way through city council. Ironically, the Civic Arena turned out to be too large, too unwieldy for live theater. This facility didn't come into its own until 1964 when the Beatles brought electronically amplified rock — and very large crowds — to Pittsburgh.

This was Pittsburgh's first public high school. Central High had opened in rented rooms on Smithfield Street (where the Mellon Bank building is now) in 1855. Due to expanded enrollment, the city erected this facility on the bluff overlooking the Pennsylvania Station in 1871. Expanded enrollment forced another move in 1916 to the new Schenley High School. For a time this building housed a business high school. It was demolished in 1946.

By the 1870's more than 750,000 Catholics lived in the Pittsburgh area, many of German descent. Six Holy Ghost priests, banished from Germany for political reasons, settled in this area and established the Pittsburgh Catholic College of the Holy Ghost. This institution of higher learning opened in 1878 on the second floor of a commercial building located in the area where the Civic Arena stands today. Tuition was six dollars a month. When enrollment increased, the fathers moved their school to permanent quarters on the nearby Bluff, an elevated stretch of land overlooking the Mon river. This postcard shows the first building erected by the fathers, the Administration Building, dedicated in 1885.

After achieving university status in 1911, the school changed its name to Duquesne University of the Holy Ghost. Aside from its academic credentials, Duquesne University is celebrated for its internationally renowned troupe of folk dancers, the Tamburitzans, and for its basketball team, the Duquesne Dukes, whose tradition of athletic accomplishment dates back to 1922.

Pittsburg College, Pittsburg, Pa.

In the early 1840's philanthropist crusader Dorathea Dix, noted mostly for her work on behalf of the mentally ill, visited Pittsburgh and discovered there was not so much as a single hospital in the entire city. She wrote a scathing report to the Commonwealth of Pennsylvania, excerpts from which were printed in the local press. This shamed the citizens of Pittsburgh into action. Bishop O'Connor used his pulpit at St. Paul's Church to raise money for a hospital. O'Connor's Sisters of Mercy used the money raised to open a small facility in rented rooms on Penn Avenue, downtown. They called this "The Mercy." By 1848 the sisters had acquired a small three-story building on Stephenson Street on what is now called the Lower Hill. The original building offered sixty beds. Mercy Hospital expanded many times over the years, as is evidenced by this 1910 postcard.

When Henry Clay Frick was shot by anarchist Alexander Berkman, he was taken to Mercy Hospital for emergency treatment. Grateful for the quality of care he received, he left $5,000,000 to the hospital in his will.

Pittsburgh, Pa. Mercy Hospital

PITTSBURGH'S SMARTEST NIGHT CLUB

HARLEM CASINO — 1714 CENTRE AVE. — PITTSBURGH, PA.

The Hill District was to Pittsburgh jazz what Harlem was to New York jazz. The greatest black performers of the 1920's and 1930's played at clubs here. Often, an early evening performance at the more staid supper clubs downtown preceded going uptown to the Hill for the real show between 1 and 4 a.m. For many years, The Harlem Casino was the premiere legitimate "sepia entertainment" club in the Hill. (There were numerous illegally operated clubs, especially during Prohibition.)

This linen card from the 1930's was an advertising card. On the back, this message is printed in script simulating handwriting: "Oh, Boy! What a time we had here last night. The show was swell and the music real swingy. Best sepia entertainment I've ever seen—wish you could have enjoyed it with us. If ever you get a chance don't miss an opportunity to see Harlem in swing." Unfortunately, Pittsburgh's smartest night club is no longer in operation.

In 1818, Charles K. Kenny purchased the land where Kennywood Park now stands for "five pounds, ten shillings, six pence and a barrel of whiskey." The original farmhouse site on Kenny Farm became a popular picnic spot with Mr. Kenny's blessing and was soon known as Kenny's Grove. Toward the end of the 19th century, rail companies built amusement parks and picnic groves at the end of railcar lines to increase ridership on weekends and evenings. In 1898, the Monongahela Street Railways

Pavilion in Kennywood Park.

Company, under Andrew W. Mellon, rented Kenny's Grove to build a park. Mr. Mellon named it "Kennywood" and claimed that it rivaled Schenley Park for scenic beauty. Most trolley parks had only picnic benches, a bandstand, and a carousel; but Kennywood was an amusement resort similar to Coney Island.

This card shows part of the midway. The center left building with the dome and the neo-Roman columns was the funhouse, known then as the Daffy Dilla.

The "Racer," Kennywood Park.

Kennywood's claim to fame is its roller coasters. The first coaster was a "Gravity Ride"—a primitive, short ride with cars that, in the absence of electricity, were hauled to the top of their first peak by very burly men. This coaster was replaced in 1902 with the park's first figure-eight coaster, built by Pittsburgh's Ingersoll brothers, creators of many fine amusement rides at Kennywood, West View, and Fred Ingersoll's own Luna Park. The Ingersolls built the first version of The Racer (shown here) for Kennywood in 1910. In 1974, Kennywood became nationally known when coaster enthusiast Robert Cartmell published an article in *The New York Times* proclaiming that Kennywood's Thunderbolt was "the ultimate coaster."

RUSTIC BRIDGE AT KENNYWOOD PARK, PITTSBURG, PA.

A wonderful, country-style bridge made of logs and branches that led to the dance pavilion—now gone.

Confluence of Allegheny and Monongahela Rivers forming the Ohio River, Exposition Buildings on the "Point," Pittsburg, Pa.

Across the Allegheny River from the old Exposition is a stadium called Exposition Park. After the north shore Exposition burned to the ground in 1883, the Pittsburgh Baseball Club purchased the land, and created a field and bleachers for the budding Pittsburgh Pirates. Named Exposition Park in memory of the former Allegheny Exposition, it was not associated in any way with the Exposition at The Point.

Some people argue that the first World Series was played in here in 1903 — the first time the National League champions, the Pittsburgh Pirates, squared off against the Boston Red Sox, division leaders of the new American League. In 1904, John McGraw, manager of the National League champion New York Giants, refused to play the division title holders from the American League, saying, "Let them get reputations first." The next year, World Series competition resumed, leading to the argument that the first World Series was played in 1905. (Pittsburgh lost that 1903 contest — 5 games to 3.)

ALONG WATER STREET, PITTSBURG. FOUR SQUARES FROM JUNCTION OF THE ALLEGHENY AND MONONGAHELA.

BOATING AT THE ENTRANCE TO BASE BALL PARK. ALLEGHENY.

Greatest flood ever recorded in Allegheny county. Mononaghela river guaging 36.2 ft. of water, and Allegheny river 36.6 ft. Next greatest flood, the celebrated "Pumpkin Flood" of 1832, followed by the 1884 flood, which was 3.3 ft. less.

This may be the only postcard showing the entrance to Exposition Park—a flood card from 1907.

Federal Street Bridge, looking East,
Pittsburgh, Pa.

The first Sixth Street Bridge opened to the public in 1820 where the Robinson family, one of the first families to settle in Allegheny, had operated a successful ferry business. Constructed of wood, it was the first bridge between Pittsburgh and the town of Allegheny. Horse-drawn trolleys in the 1850's required a bigger, stronger bridge; so Roebling built one of his wire suspension bridges at Sixth Street in 1857.

Here is the third Sixth Street Bridge. The two camel-back spans were a familiar sight in Pittsburgh from 1892 until 1927 when a fourth bridge was needed. But the county decided that the superbly designed, camel-backed spans could be used for a bridge down river in Coraopolis. Each span was lowered, using eight 500-ton jacks, onto barges. To clear the Manchester Bridge at The Point, fourteen feet of the top arch of the truss was dismantled and rebuilt later at Neville Island before being moved to Coraopolis. The county saved about $350,000 by recycling this bridge.

After the English took The Point in 1758, white settlers moved north across the Allegheny River. Indians in this area (Federal Street was originally an Indian trail) chased most settlers back to Pittsburgh or killed them. After the Indian wars, a few families moved into this hilly, rough area. In 1787, the State of Pennsylvania surveyed the land across the Allegheny River to lay out the town of Allegheny for the county seat of the new Allegheny County. The surveyor, Mr. David Redick, characterized the land as ". . . more suitable for residents of the moon." Nonetheless, he laid out a section for public buildings and a Commons area where future residents could graze their cattle. The area developed into a borough in 1823 and a city in 1840. Allegheny became a successful business center, rivaling her sister city across the river. Cotton and wool industries caught on first, then iron and glass manufacturing. Later came forges, tanneries, saw mills, breweries, and brick-making operations. City Hall, pictured in this

City Hall. Allegheny, Pa.

Made in Germany.   145.

postcard, was built in 1864 and housed Allegheny's police and fire departments, post office, and administrative offices. This City Hall was later torn down to make way for the Buhl Planetarium.

Alleghenians fought off annexation by Pittsburgh several times; but in 1907, after a public vote between the two cities where the majority vote won (Pittsburgh had more voters), Allegheny City became officially, if reluctantly, annexed to the city of Pittsburgh.

Western Pennsylvania
Penitentiary, North Side,
Pittsburg, Pa.

Most of the Allegheny County offices ended up in Pittsburgh. The town of Allegheny did, however, host the County Penitentiary. The first penitentiary, built in 1827, was in the West Commons where the Aviary stands today. In 1886, the second and current penitentiary, pictured here, was built along the Ohio River in the Woods Run area. It shows the influence of H. H. Richardson's Romanesque style, popular in the years following the building of the Allegheny County Courthouse.

The Fort Wayne Depot, North Side,
Pittsburgh, Pa.

In the 1850's two railroad lines—the Ohio and Pennsylvania; and the Pittsburgh, Fort Wayne, and Chicago—operated out of stations located in Allegheny City's lower Federal Street area. This station was built between 1905-1906 and was conveniently situated halfway between downtown Pittsburgh and the Allegheny City business district. The Fort Wayne was a frequently used commuter station for many years, serving people in the Sewickley and Quaker Valley areas. When rail transportation fell in popularity, the Fort Wayne became a ghost station. It is gone now.

View showing Carnegie Hall,
City Hall and Post Office,
N. S., Pittsburgh, Pa.

In 1850, James Anderson, founder of Allegheny City's first iron works, opened his personal library to young working men. On Saturdays, he worked in the library himself, offering guidance to the young men who made use of his collection—among them, Andrew Carnegie and Henry Phipps. Toward the end of his business career, Carnegie remembered Colonel Anderson and his library, and decided to create free libraries as gifts to the public. The first Carnegie Free Library opened in Braddock in 1889; it was endowed by Carnegie, not supported by public taxes.

The library pictured here opened in 1890 on Federal Street in Allegheny City. This time, Carnegie donated the building with the stipulation that Allegheny support the library with tax revenues. This card shows a stretch of East Ohio Street that doesn't exist any more. Next to the Library are the City Hall and the Old Post Office.

West Park, now West Allegheny Commons, North Side, was initially a bare, rock-strewn commons used for grazing cattle. As Allegheny City prospered, wealthy businessmen built their homes around its perimeter. They wanted it to be developed into an attractive area with trees, flowers, and shrubbery. In 1867, West Park with formally landscaped gardens became the first public park west of the Allegheny Mountains.

A Cool Spot, West Park, Allegheny, Penn.

Allegheny, Pa., Allegheny Park.

In 1893, a lake was built in the center of West Park. Named Lake Elizabeth after then-Mayor Kirschler's daughter, it covered more than two acres. Ducks and white swans graced its waters. Children of the rich sailed little boats in it, their coachmen in attendance. In the winter, ice skaters could stop for a quick warm-up by bonfires scattered throughout the park. Refreshments were available. Scottish residents entertained everyone with "curling," played at the Irwin Avenue end of the lake.

Eventually, children of the "rougher element" moved in on the lake. They stole the swan and duck eggs, swam naked, even beat up the rich kids, pushing their coachmen into the water. City officials responded to complaints by remodelling the lake into a public pool. The beautiful bathhouse in the background was built around the same time the lake was converted (perhaps to encourage modesty?).

Lake Elizabeth remained a pool until the late 1930's when health officials, pointing out the dangers of swimming in stagnant water, had it drained and filled in. During World War II, this spot was a dumping ground for metal pots donated to the war effort. With the North Side redevelopment program of the 1960's, the Department of Parks and Recreations rebuilt a shallower, smaller lake and named it West Commons Lake. North Siders still call it Lake Elizabeth.

Bathing at Lake Elizabeth, North Side, Pittsburgh, Pa.

This card shows two Allegheny Park fountains. The bottom one was in the North Park part of the quadrangle across from where the current Allegheny General Hospital is located.

This was another elegant public fountain near Allegheny Park. It was located in the Public Square that bordered the Allegheny Post Office, City Hall, and Carnegie Library (background).

Lake Elizabeth in its heyday. This card is postmarked July 10th, 1911.

West Park was one of a quadrangle of parks known as Allegheny Park. This fountain near the Elks' Temple was in East Park (now East Commons).

Allegheny City was rich with fountains early in this century, but after it was absorbed into Pittsburgh, all of its fountains were removed. Pittsburgh claimed it lacked funds to maintain them.

Washington Monument.

Hampton Monument, Allegheny Park, Pittsburgh, Pa.

The equestrian sculpture with George Washington was unveiled at a George Washington birthday celebration in 1891. The father and son cannon in the foreground no longer appears with the monument. This work was commissioned by the Junior Order of United American Mechanics.

The Hampton Battery Memorial (bottom) honors the Pennsylvania Independent Light Artillery, Battery F, and their first captain, Robert B. Hampton. Of its 80+ members who fought in the Civil War, only 28 survived. With funding help from private citizens and the city of Allegheny, these men raised the sculpture onto its pedestal in May, 1871, without a formal ceremony. The Spanish-made cannon, captured in Cuba in 1888, was added in 1899.

This was the first Phipps Conservatory, built by Andrew Carnegie's business partner, Henry Phipps, in the West Park section of Allegheny City in 1887. It was an immediate success, despite some initial disagreement between Presbyterian and Lutheran ministers over Mr. Phipps' stipulation that the conservatory must be open on Sunday—the only day most working people had off. The Lutherans agreed with Phipps; the Presbyterians wanted the facility closed on Sundays. The Presbyterians were forced to relent when a Lutheran minister caught a Presbyterian minister visiting the conservatory on a Sunday. In 1927, a gas explosion damaged this conservatory. The city razed what remained of the building in 1949.

Phipps Conservatory, Allegheny Park, North Side, Pittsburg, Pa.

Dating from the grand period of U. S. government buildings, this Italian Renaissance structure with its great central dome opened in 1898 in Allegheny City. When Pittsburgh and Allegheny merged, this became the North Side branch of the postal service It functioned as such until the 1960's when an urban redevelopment program slated the Old Post Office for demolition. At that point a relatively new preservation group, the Pittsburgh History and Landmarks Foundation, stepped in. They raised the money to purchase the building from the Urban Redevelopment Authority. It was restored and then adapted for use as a Pittsburgh and Allegheny County Museum. Today the Old Post Office is home to an innovative children's museum.

Post Office, ALLEGHANY, Pa.   3038

The old Allegheny Market House was built in 1863 and bordered Allegheny City's beautiful public square. This Romanesque building was the heart of public life in Allegheny City. Branching out in all directions from the Market House were small businesses—hat shops, old-fashioned five and tens, ethnic delicatessens, taverns, dress shops, schools for specialized training, and drug stores with Art Deco soda fountains that served vanilla Cokes. North Siders referred to this area as "downtown." Crossing over the 6th or 7th Street Bridge to enter Pittsburgh meant going "over-town."

The author remembers the Market House as more than a place to get locally grown produce and fresh meat; it was a small-scale Harrods. The razing of the Market House and the surrounding business district to build a concrete mall was the final bomb dropped on old Allegheny City. The distinction between downtown and over-town disappeared within a year.

North Side Market House, Pittsburgh, Pa.

The Buhl Planetarium was a combination planetarium and popular science museum. After visitors were seated inside the domed room of the planetarium, a Zeiss projector rose from the floor to project a moving map of the stars upon the surface of the dome. Visitors seemed to be standing on the observation deck of a spaceship, looking out into the galaxy. Outside the domed room were galleries featuring popular science exhibits. The Buhl Planetarium was created as a living memorial to Henry Buhl, Jr., co-founder of old Allegheny's popular Boggs and Buhl Department Store. Although the building still stands, it no longer functions as a planetarium.

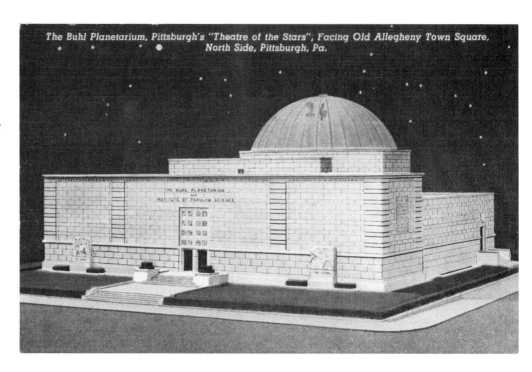

The Buhl Planetarium, Pittsburgh's "Theatre of the Stars", Facing Old Allegheny Town Square, North Side, Pittsburgh, Pa.

The first high school graduates in Allegheny City completed a two-year program in 1879. Classes were held in a small building that had been a planing (wood) mill during the Civil War and later housed a cigar factory. Once education caught on in Allegheny, there were far more students than the little planing mill could accommodate. James S. Young, an attorney in Allegheny, spearheaded the campaign to build this towered building, which opened in 1889. It was considered the finest schoolhouse west of the Allegheny Mountains. Regretfully, this playful Romanesque building was demolished in the 1930's. Mary Roberts Rinehart graduated from Allegheny High School, and Willa Cather taught English there.

Copyright 1905 by the Rotograph Co.
5787   High School, Allegheny, Pa.

This first Allegheny General Hospital, created and endowed by local philanthropists, opened on Stockton Avenue in 1886. It featured five wards, several private rooms, and a school for nurses. As Pittsburgh grew, the need for hospital services expanded beyond the capacity of this tiny facility. In 1936, Allegheny General opened a new "skyscraper hospital" nearby. This new facility enjoys a first-rate reputation, both locally and nationally. Old timers say, however, that this first Allegheny General was known locally as "The Butcher Shop."

This Presbyterian Hospital, on the border of Allegheny Park, opened in 1895 to serve all religious affiliations. The Presbyterians moved their hospital to other quarters in 1929. Today, this facility is part of the Catholic Church's Divine Providence Hospital.

Memorial Hall, Western
Theological Seminary,
North Side, Pittsburgh, Pa.

The Presbyterians founded The Western Theological Seminary in 1825 and assumed the responsibility of "inspiring and training capable young men to preach the gospel and serve as efficient church workers."

This structure was built between 1911-1912 and replaced an older dormitory building erected in 1877 by Dr. C. C. Beatty in memory of his beloved wife (thus, the name "Memorial Hall"). Today, it is part of the Community College of Allegheny County and is known as West Hall. The Western Theological Seminary still inspires and trains students in the East End of the city.

Henry John Heinz was born to German immigrant parents in 1844. Anna Heinz required her children to work in the family garden; H. J. sold surplus produce to neighboring households. As a teen, he bottled horseradish from the family garden and sold it along with the fresh produce to his regular customers and, later, to grocers and hotel keepers—hence, the beginning of the H. J. Heinz Company.

Constructed in 1890-1898, the complex pictured here was the "House of the 57 Varieties." In addition to the food processing plant and offices, the complex contained a gymnasium, natatorium, auditorium, library with reading rooms, and medical facilities for employees. Horses were very important to the Heinz company. There was a three-story horse hotel that included an equestrian hospital, a turkish bath, and a roof garden for horses who needed to take a little air.

View from Troy Hill, showing H. J. Heinz Plant, Pittsburgh, Pa.

This advertising card pictures a Saturnesque world with processed foods floating atop its ring. Lighted emblems bearing the famous 57 Varieties logo indicate the location of Heinz plants throughout the world. For many years, the Heinz Company was best known for its pickles. During the 1893 Chicago World's Fair, the Heinz Company's exhibit wasn't well attended. Heinz then instructed his employees to canvass the Fair grounds, handing out cards that advertised a free souvenir. Soon, the Heinz exhibit was overwhelmed with visitors. The souvenir? A ceramic pickle with a hook in the back to be worn as a lapel pin. During the course of the World's Fair, the Heinz Company gave out over a million pickle pins.

Courtesy of H. J. Heinz Company

Allegheny Cemetery, in the Lawrenceville area, opened in 1844 and was the first "park-style" cemetery in the Pittsburgh area and the fourth such cemetery in the U. S. In the 19th century, a graveyard was a place to visit, take a stroll, or have a family outing. Gravestones were fashioned as works of art and featured poetic inscriptions that conveyed a sense of who the person was, what he did, or what peculiar or untimely way he might have died.

The Superintendent of such a cemetery was considered an important, prestigious person. Allegheny Cemetery's first Superintendent was John Chislett—Pittsburgh's most prominent architect in 1844. Hundreds of people important to Pittsburgh history are buried in Allegheny Cemetery, among them Stephen Collins Foster, Lillian Russell, Ebenezer Denny (first Mayor of Pittsburgh), John Neville, James Scott Negley, Christopher Lyman Magee, Joseph Horne, and the notorious Mr. Harry K. Thaw.

Entrance to Allegheny Cemetery,   Pittsburg, Pa.

The United States Allegheny Arsenal was established in 1814 in Lawrenceville on ground purchased from William Foster, father of Stephen Collins Foster. It provided ammunition for the Union during the Civil War. Among other things, the Arsenal was famous for a tremendous gunpowder explosion that occurred there in 1862. At first thought to be the work of Confederate conspirators, the explosion was later discovered to have been accidental. Nearly eighty people were killed and many more wounded — the most deadly accident in Pittsburgh history.

This card shows the fortress-like entrance to the Arsenal (top) and the Main Arsenal Building where small arms were stored (bottom). The Arsenal ceased operations in 1901. Both buildings pictured here are gone.

Entrance to
Allegheny Arsenal,
Pittsburgh, Pa.

Building No. 19. Allegheny Arsenal,
Pittsburgh, Pa.

In 1800 Father Suibertus Mollinger, who came from a wealthy family, built this chapel in Troy Hill as a shrine to St. Anthony of Padua. Because of political and religious upheaval in Italy and Germany, he was able to acquire one of the world's largest collection of relics — over 5,000 objects — for St. Anthony's Chapel. These relics include a shred of the Sacred Winding Sheet, a Particle of the True Cross, the complete skeletal bones of St. Demetrius, and the skulls of martyrs St. Macharius, St. Stephana, and St. Theodore. There are also relics of John the Baptist, Mary Magdalene, St. Stephen, and St. Anthony, himself.

St. Anthony's has received national exposure recently as the set for several Hollywood feature films and TV movies.

Courtesy of Dale E. Röös

The Chapel, Riverview Park,
North Side, Pittsburgh, Pa

Allegheny City's West Park was the envy of Pittsburghers for years. When Schenley Park opened in 1889, Pittsburgh then had an enormous park with rolling hills and picnic grounds. Allegheny wanted an equivalent expanse of rolling hills for a "City Beautiful" park and bought the Watson Farm, originally owned by Samuel Watson, one of the first settlers in Allegheny. Troy Hill's leading entrepreneur, Paul Ober of the Eberhardt and Ober Brewery, sponsored the purchase. It was christened Riverview Park and presented to the city of Allegheny in July, 1894. This card shows an early shelter.

The Zoo in Riverview Park, North Side,
Pittsburgh, Pa.

Riverview Park had a respectable zoo at one time, as shown in this post-1906 card. Eventually, it was deemed excessive for one city to have two zoos, so the animals from the Riverview zoo were moved to the Highland Park facility. Stones from the bear pit of this zoo were used to build the foundation of the Bear Pit Picnic Shelter.

Allegheny Observatory, Riverview Park, Pittsburgh, Pa.

The first observatory in the Pittsburgh area was built in Allegheny City near the Federal Street end of Perrysville Avenue in 1860. This larger facility was built between 1900-1912 in Riverview Park. Samuel Pierpont Langley, an astronomer who specialized in studying the sun, brought the Allegheny Observatory to prominence with the financial support of industrialist William Thaw. The Observatory is best known for creating the Allegheny Time System—wherein the Observatory supplied exact time information to City Hall, railroads, and other businesses. Pittsburgh was the first city in the country to be synchronized. The Allegheny Time System was adopted by the United States Naval Observatory and became a national standard.

PHOTOGRAPHIC REFRACTOR ALLEGHENY OBSERVATORY
PITTSBURGH PENNSYLVANIA
46 FEET LONG   30 INCH LENS

John A. Brashear, friend and colleague of Samuel Pierpont Langley, was a gifted lens maker—at one time, the finest lens maker in the world. William Thaw acted again as benefactor by supplying Brashear with enough money to quit his "day job" as a millworker and establish his own lens-making business. Brashear designed the lens for this telescope, and was once the largest photographic refractor in the United States. It is named the Thaw Memorial Telescope, in honor of the Observatory's devoted benefactor, and is housed within the main dome.

Main Entrance and Bridge leading to West View Park, North Side, Pittsburgh, Pa.

This postcard shows the entrance to West View Park, an amusement park opened by T. M. Harton in 1906 on drained swamp land in the new borough of West View. The T. M. Harton Company built and operated carousels, roller coasters, and other amusement rides in parks throughout the country. (For a time, the Harton Company operated a carousel and a scenic train ride on grounds owned by the Western Exposition at The Point.) West View was a large, elegant park surrounded by trees with picnic grounds and a lake for boating. It was the showcase of the Harton Company.

West View Park, North Side, Pittsburg, Pa.

An early card showing the entrance to The Mystic Chute, one of the first rides in West View Park. Riders were pulled in a car to the top of an incline and then released down into a body of water. The entrance to the Pony Drive is in the foreground. The squat, safari hat-shaped building in the center was a refreshment stand. The domed building behind the refreshment stand housed the Harton Company carousel. To the right of the carousel was West View's first Penny Arcade.

The midway in the early 1910's. The park opened with a figure-eight roller coaster. In 1910, the Harton Company built a coaster using radical, new engineering designs. It was an elongated ride, stretching over the entire length of Lake Placid and featuring an extremely sharp, angled dip of over fifty feet. This ride was called the "Dip the Dip" and, later, "The Dips." It can be seen in this card in the left background behind the Mystic Chute.

This card shows the length of the Dip the Dip ride. Lake Placid was a man-made body of water. At the turn of the century, every park had a lake or a pool. Strolling along the shore and boating were popular pastimes.

West View was built in a swamp-like ravine that was surrounded by beautiful, wooded hills. This is one of the more scenic stretches of the Pony Drive.

West View's Dance Pavilion was an open air design so that people outside could watch the people inside and vice versa. The pavilion's ballroom was the most popular dance spot in Pittsburgh throughout most of its existence. Big bands played here in the 1920's and 1930's. Local radio stations broadcast live from the ballroom during the summer; some programs were aired over national radio. During the Depression, dancing at the Pavilion kept the park in the black. In the late 1940's, the Pavilion was rebuilt in an Art Deco style and renamed "Danceland." Unfortunately, an eight-alarm fire burned it to the ground in 1973, hastening the demise of West View. In 1977, the park closed for good.

Entrance and Driveway, Schenley Park, Pittsburgh, Pa.

In the 1850's, cities started to provide free recreational facilities to their citizens. New York City, Philadelphia, Boston, and Chicago developed park systems by setting aside stretches of land within the city where residents could get away from their apartments, neighborhoods, and jobs to relax. Pittsburgh, one of the most crowded cities in the East, thought that parks were a nice idea but an unaffordable luxury. Edward Manning Bigelow, very influential in city government at that time, envisioned a Pittsburgh luxuriant with park lands. Large tracts of land in the east were still undeveloped, the largest and most suitable of which was originally owned by James O'Hara and now belonged to Mary Schenley, O'Hara's granddaughter. This card shows the entrance to Schenley Park.

Forbes and Darlington Entrance to Schenley Park, Pittsburg, Pa.

When Pittsburgh's Mary Croghan was a fourteen-year-old girl at boarding school, she met forty-six-year-old military man and adventurer Captain E. H. Schenley. They secretly married and escaped to England. Mary Schenley returned to Pittsburgh only a few times to deal with her estate. When Bigelow tried to buy land from her, City Council wouldn't pay the price. Bigelow later tried to have Mary Schenley's property condemned so that the city could take her property without remuneration, but Mary was too smart and too rich to fall victim to this scheme. Remarkably, she didn't hold this against Bigelow in later dealings.

This card shows a second entrance to the park located along Forbes Avenue.

In 1888, Bigelow became the city's first Director of Public Works. He arranged for Mary Schenley's Pittsburgh lawyer, Robert Carnahan, who supported Bigelow's park system idea, to visit her in England. He implored her to consider how important a park would be to the working people of Pittsburgh. She reflected upon how much Hyde Park, which bordered her residence, had meant to her. She and agreed to donate several hundred acres of her Pittsburgh estate for the development of a park. In 1889, the city received three hundred acres from Mrs.

Panther Hollow Bridge, Pittsburg, Pa.

24747

Schenley and took an option to buy one hundred more. Schenley Park opened to the public shortly thereafter. This card shows the Panther Hollow Bridge entrance to the park.

This photographic card shows afternoon boaters on Panther Hollow Lake by Panther Hollow Bridge. The building across the lake is the boathouse. Bordering the lake was a tiny community known as "Little Italy." Businesses included a barber shop, grocery store, and a steamship agency (for visits to and from Italy). Dairy farming was the mainstay of Little Italy, and cattle grazed in and around the lake area up until the 1940's.

This rare card shows an Italianesque fountain popular in many Edwardian English gardens. The fountain is gone now.

The Schenley Oval, now used as a track field, was originally a race track. The grandstand, left, was replaced by tennis courts.

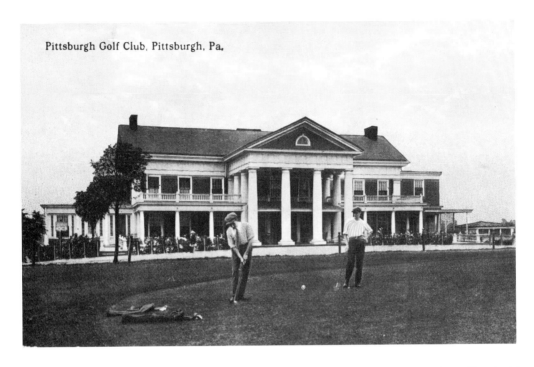

Pittsburgh Golf Club, Pittsburgh, Pa.

The Pittsburgh Golf Club, a private country club still headquartered in the building behind the golfers in this card, originally created the golf course in Schenley Park for its members. The city took over the course and turned it into a public facility, making the Pittsburgh Golf Club the only country club in the area without its own golf course. Rumors said that Christopher L. Magee urged the city to take over the course when he was refused admission to the club.

SERPENTINE DRIVE, SCHENLEY PARK.   PITTSBURGH. PA.   8068

Trees now border this roadway. When this picture was taken, much of the surrounding area was undeveloped.

Indian Spring, Schenley Park,
Pittsburgh, Pa.

This shot of the Indian Spring in Schenley Park includes the Neill Log House, one of Pittsburgh's oldest standing structures. When the Neill Log House was built in the late 1700's, this part of Pittsburgh was still pioneer land. The cabin was built with squared and fitted logs for strength and durability. The windows are small and shuttered, and the door is substantial enough to protect against Indian attack.

The Indian leader featured on the monument in the foreground was Catahecassa, which means "Black Foot" in Shawnee. He led not only his own tribe, but a confederation of Indians in the battle against the expansion of the white man into their homelands, particularly west of the Allegheny Mountains. In 1795, a peace treaty was signed with the Indian confederacy. Thereafter, Catahecassa committed himself to preserving peace between the white man and the Indian.

Magee Memorial,
Schenley Park,
Pittsburg, Pa.

This granite and bronze memorial by Augustus Saint-Gaudens stands across from the entrance to the Carnegie Free Library in Oakland. It honors Christopher Lyman Magee, famous in Pittsburgh history for creating a political ring that dominated commercial and political life in this city for seventeen uninterrupted years. As a young man he studied political rings in Philadelphia and New York in order to create the perfect one in Pittsburgh. Along with the politico/entrepreneur William Flynn, Magee used influence, bribery, ballot stuffing, and blackmail to route millions of private and taxpayer dollars to businesses associated with the ring. Religious leaders, citizens' groups, and honest politicians were unable to destroy the ring, despite numerous attempts. It ended only with Magee's death in 1901.

This graceful memorial features Charity holding an overflowing cornucopia and bears an inscription from Shakespeare's *The Merchant of Venice*. It reads, "The Quality of Mercy is Not Strain'd. It droppeth as the gentle rain from heaven, Upon the Place beneath. It is twice Blessed. It blesseth Him that gives and Him that Takes."

524   BIGELOW MONUMENT, PITTSBURGH, PA

This sculpture of the hero of Pittsburgh's public park system, Edward Manning Bigelow, is located in Schenley Drive between Phipp's Conservatory and Flagstaff Hill. The pedestal is made of granite while the nine-foot figure is cast of bronze. The design is by Giuseppe Moretti, a sculptor brought to Pittsburgh by Bigelow to create works of art for the new park system. The Bigelow Monument was dedicated on July 4, 1895. Mr. Bigelow had the rare honor of attending the dedication of his own monument.

The success of Allegheny City's conservatory inspired Henry Phipps to build another, greater conservatory for Pittsburgh. The second Phipps Conservatory, located in Schenley Park, opened with an exhibit of exotic plants acquired from the Chicago World's Fair. The conservatory flourished under the direction of George W. Burke, Superintendent of City Parks. After Burke's death, however, park-related positions became a matter of political appointment rather than expertise. The conservatory declined to near dereliction. The rare plants and trees died and were replaced with rubber trees, red croton, and common house plants. A 1930's newspaper noted that rats scuttled along the conservatory's worn, overgrown paths; lice and insects ran riot; and the building needed to be condemned. Bulbs for the Spring Flower Show were delivered directly to the homes of prominent city council members.

This postcard shows the Phipps Conservatory in its earliest days.

Phipps Conservatory, Schenley Park, Pittsburg, Pa.

The original stone entrance to the Phipps Conservatory followed the Romanesque style of architect H. H. Richardson. His new courthouse and jail in downtown Pittsburgh impressed everyone, and the style then appeared on new buildings, entrances, and facades throughout the city. Although this beautiful entrance was later removed, the Pittsburgh History and Landmarks Foundation is exploring the possibility of rebuilding it as of this writing.

Entrance to Phipps Conservatory, Pittsburgh, Pa.

In 1935, Mrs. Johanna Hailman, wealthy socialite and Pittsburgh's foremost living woman artist, proclaimed to the newspapers that the Phipps Conservatory was "a filthy, rotten old sandhole." She sacrificed her annual Nassau vacation to work at the conservatory every morning at 8:30 with her own pick and shovel until late in the evening. Many of the city's wealthy and talented pitched in, and that year's Spring Flower Show was the best in the history of the conservatory. Mrs. Hailman was at the opening ceremonies to pose with the blossoms of her labor.

These days, professional horticulturists tend the exotic flora. The Spring Flower Show has met with great critical success and is now one of Pittsburgh's most celebrated annual events. This card is one of a series of 16 issued by the Pittsburgh Press; it features a turn-of-the-century flower show display.

Easter Morning in the Conservatory, Schenley Park, Pittsburg, Pa.

Andrew Carnegie contended that the wealthy had a moral commitment to use their wealth to educate, enrich, and inspire the working people of the world, thus advancing the condition of humankind. Carnegie had already created several free libraries in the Pittsburgh area when he created the Carnegie Institute, pictured here. Built by the firm of Longfellow, Alden and Harlow in 1895, it featured Pittsburgh's first Carnegie Free Library, a Music Hall, a Museum of Natural History, and an Art Gallery. This card shows the original 1895 structure. During

5098 CARNEGIE LIBRARY SHENLEY PARK. 3/9. *I wrote you last night.* PITTSBURGH, PA.
ILL. POST CARD CO., N. Y. *received your letter this afternoon.* H. H.

expansion, completed in 1907, the domes, the driveway entrance, and the Richardsonian towers were removed. In his autobiography, Carnegie wrote of the Institute: "This is my monument, because here I lived my early life and made my start, and I am today in heart a devoted son of dear old smoky Pittsburgh."

The Carnegie Museum of Natural History contains one of the largest and most spectacular paleontology collections in the world. In 1898, Carnegie financed a fossil dig in Wyoming, stipulating that whatever was discovered belonged to the Carnegie Museum. This dig produced the largest and most complete dinosaur skeleton discovered up until that time. It was named *Diplodocus carnegie* in honor of its financial benefactor. The dinosaur, pictured in this postcard, was so large that it could not be mounted until the Institute's expansion was completed in 1907. Later, the museum mounted the remains of a lady dinosaur next to the *Diplodocus carnegie* and named it *Apatosaurus louisae*, after Andrew's wife.

Interior, Carnegie Museum, Pittsburg, Pa.

46:—School of Industry, Carnegie Tech., Pittsburgh, Pa.

The evolution of Pittsburgh into a city of industry created demand for men with specialized, technical training. On November 15, 1900, at a meeting of the Board of the Carnegie Institute, Andrew Carnegie offered to contribute money for a vocational school if the city of Pittsburgh would provide a site. The Carnegie Institute would manage the school. The city provided a generous chunk of land adjacent to the Institute, part of Mary Schenley's donated acreage. The building in this postcard was Industries Hall, still under construction when the first classes were held in October, 1905. It was renamed Porter Hall in 1939.

Andrew Carnegie, a self-taught man, was skeptical of higher education. He intended the four Carnegie Technical Schools (Engineering, Industries, Arts, and the Women's School) to be strictly vocational, so early graduates did not receive degrees.

CARNEGIE INSTITUTE OF TECHNOLOGY, PITTSBURGH, PA.

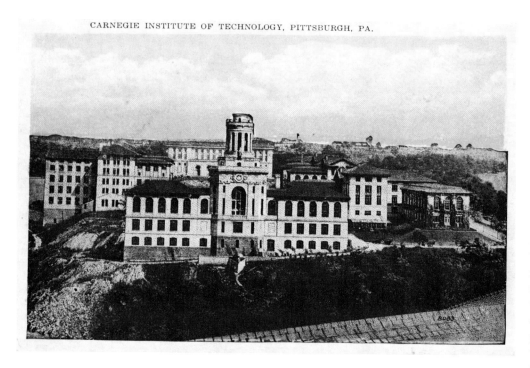

In 1912, the trustees of the Carnegie Institute incorporated as the Carnegie Institute of Technology with the power to grant degrees. The campus developed quickly, as can be seen in this 1920's postcard. On the far right is Industries Hall. The foremost building with the tower was Machinery Hall. Designed by campus architect Henry Hornbostel, this Beaux-Arts building housed the power plant used by the mechanical and electrical engineering departments; the tower was an elegant, 19th-century sheath over the plant's smokestack. The wedge-shaped object in front of Machinery Hall is the bronze bow from the armored cruiser *U. S. S. Pennsylvania*, which was decommissioned in 1912 when Machinery Hall was nearing completion. Hornbostel put the 7000-pound bow in front of Machinery Hall to suggest "a ship headed toward knowledge."

Carnegie Tech became Carnegie Mellon, a distinguished private university, in 1967 when C. I. T. merged with the Mellon Institute.

Andrew Carnegie's father was a gifted and financially successful weaver in Scotland. When mechanization took over the textile business, the Carnegie family came to America. Mechanization here, however, meant the elder Carnegie still could not support his family with his loom. During this resettlement in the States, Andrew's mother, Margaret Morrison Carnegie, worked at all hours, skillfully managed what little they had, and instilled moral values in her sons. In her honor, Andrew created the Margaret Morrison

Margaret Morrison, Carnegie School, Pittsburg, Pa.

Carnegie College, a vocational school for young women. Departments taught household economics, clothing design, secretarial skills, and general science. This postcard shows the school's 1906-1907 building. An inscription in the rotunda reads: "To make and inspire the home; to lesson suffering and increase happiness; to aid mankind in its upward struggles; to ennoble and adorn life's work, however humble. These are women's high prerogatives."

MELLON INSTITUTE, UNIVERSITY OF PITTSBURGH, PITTSBURGH, PA.

The Mellon Institute was the brain child of Dr. Robert Kennedy Duncan, who wanted to link scientific inquiry with industrial research. Through the "application of modern science to industry," Dr. Duncan expected the world to enter "an era of gracious living." He arrived in Pittsburgh in 1910, and University of Pittsburgh trustees Andrew W. and Richard B. Mellon

financially helped Duncan establish the Mellon Institute in 1913. It was the first industrial research center in the nation. The building in this postcard, the first building created specifically to house the Institute, was built in 1915. The Mellon Institute was part of the University of Pittsburgh until 1927 when it incorporated separately.

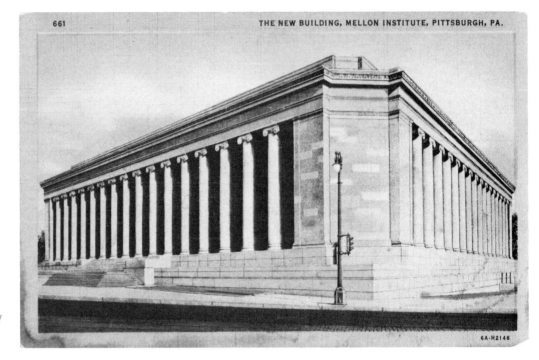

661   THE NEW BUILDING, MELLON INSTITUTE, PITTSBURGH, PA.

6A-H2146

The work done at the Mellon Institute expanded over the years, creating the need for additional space. This card shows the second building created specifically to house the Institute. This massive structure features 62 Greek columns made of limestone, each weighing 60 tons. These columns are so large that special routing was created to get them through Pittsburgh's narrow streets and tight corners. In 1967, Mellon Institute merged with Carnegie Tech to create Carnegie-Mellon University.

DOUBLE DECK CAR, PITTSBURGH, PA.   LARGEST IN THE WORLD, SEATS 110 PEOPLE.

The Pittsburgh Railways Company built the first double-decker 6000 series trolley in 1912. Back then it took a crew of men to operated a traction car; double-deckers were created to increase the number of passengers per crew. This trolley seated 110 people. However, on holidays more than 200 people could be crammed into the 6000. Double-deckers ran mostly on the Highland Avenue routes. They were retired in 1924.

Exterior Duquesne Garden, Pittsburg, Pa.

In 1890, the Duquesne Traction Company built this stately building on the corner of Fifth Avenue and Craig Street as a "car barn" for horse-drawn trolleys. Within a few years, the switch to electrically powered trolleys meant that traction magnate C. L. Magee possessed a building with no purpose. Around this same time Pittsburgh's first indoor skating rink, the Casino, opened in the Oakland area. It was enormously popular until ammonia in the Casino's ice-making machine caught fire and blew up the place. Andrew McSwigan, an associate of Magee's who had assisted in developing several traction company amusement parks, suggested that the car barn might be converted into an ice-skating arena. Magee agreed, stipulating that it must be "a nice place." When it opened in 1897, over 10,000 Pittsburghers turned out to skate on the world's largest (26,000 square feet) rink. During the off season "the Gardens" sponsored boxing and tennis events. Tennis greats Tilden, Vines, and Perry played at the Gardens. In 1901, the Metropolitan Opera caused a sensation with *Tristan and Isolde*. Enrico Caruso showed up unannounced at Andrew McSwigan's office to ask to sing at the Gardens. Victor Herbert conducted his orchestra here, and John Philip Sousa did not overlook Oakland's entertainment palace. During the Depression, ex-Hollywood PR man Milt Crandall sponsored marathon dance contests at the Gardens. He got around a law prohibiting paid attractions on Sunday by packing his dancers into a truck on Saturday night, hauling them down to the Show Boat on the Allegheny River where they were outside the jurisdiction of the Pittsburgh police, and trucking them back to the Gardens on Monday. During one marathon, a mother-and-son team dragged each other around a dance floor for 23 days.

Pittsburgh, Pa., Ice Rink, Duquesne Garden.   Photo by R. W. Johnston.

The ice skating fad made hockey a popular sport. Pittsburgh had four hockey teams skating at the Gardens at one time: the Hornets, the Yellow Jackets, the Shamrocks, and the Pirates. Duquesne Gardens paid all athletes who played in their facility, whether amateur or professional. Amateur Canadian hockey players started migrating down south to Pittsburgh in order to be paid. A Canadian hockey organization plan to ban Canadian athletes who played in Pittsburgh backfired; Canadian teams turned professional in order to survive. It could be said that Duquesne Garden's "pay for play" policy lead to Pittsburgh's becoming the birthplace of professional hockey.

The Gardens experienced a tremendous drop in attendance during the Depression. In 1936 Garden's manager John J. Harris brought Norway's hot Olympic Gold Medalist, Sonja Henii, to skate at the Gardens. This was front-page news in Pittsburgh. Fifteen thousand people were turned away. Harris started presenting skating shows at the Gardens, called "The Ice Follies." This evolved into "The Ice Capades." The Duquesne Garden, or "Gardens," as it was popularly called, was demolished in 1956 to clear space for an apartment building.

A Pittsburgh charter for the Shriners was granted in 1877. Meetings were initially held at the old Library Hall in downtown Pittsburgh. The Shriners broke ground for this Oakland facility, the Syria Mosque, in 1915 on land purchased from the estate of Mary Schenley. The public auditorium had the largest seating capacity of any facility in Pittsburgh in 1916. For many years the Mosque was home to the Pittsburgh Symphony Orchestra.

Inscriptions around the top of the building and over the windows were made from plaster models of old Arabic script. The window inscription was from the Koran and read, "There Is No Conqueror But God." The inscription under the roof was from an ancient Narkbi poem dated A.D. 1353-60: "Thou hast risen on the horizon of the kingdom of mercy to disperse what there was of dark oppression and injustice." The Syria Mosque was demolished in 1991.

SYRIA MOSQUE, PITTSBURGH, PA.

In the early 1800's, Oakland was primarily farm land. About 1850, two developers named Rice and Dithridge purchased part of Neville Craig's farm and laid out streets with names such as Craig, Neville, and Dithridge. Small homes were built there. Known as East Pittsburgh, then Bellefield, this area was one of Pittsburgh's first suburbs. Later, Andrew Carnegie built his library,

Masonic Temple, Pittsburgh Athletic Club and University Club, Pittsburgh, Pa.

music hall, and museum here. Phipps built his conservatory at the entrance to the new Schenley Park. Before long, the little houses disappeared, and massive architectural structures took their place.

This card illustrates Oakland's transition from suburb to cultural center. In the lower right is a suburban home, which is gone now, although its lawn is part of the grounds outside the Cathedral of Learning. Just across the street stands Pittsburgh's exclusive men's club, the P. A. A. To its right is the monolithic Masonic Temple.

In the late 1800's, developer Franklin Nicola purchased a portion of Mary Schenley's old farm property to build a civic cultural center. Stock in Nicola's Bellefield Company was sold to a number of people including Andrew Mellon, Henry Buhl, William Thaw, and Mary Schenley, herself. The Hotel Schenley, pictured here, functioned as the heart of Nicola's cultural center. Hotel manager Sidney Benedito, originally from New Orleans, set a tone of easy, gracious living for the Schenley. Guests of this premier Pittsburgh hotel included Sarah Bernhardt, Vaslav Nijinsky, Enrico Caruso, Teddy Roosevelt, Woodrow Wilson, and many others. This property became part of the University of Pittsburgh in 1956.

Hotel Schenley, Pittsburgh, Pa.

This is the entrance to old Forbes Field, home of the Pittsburgh Pirates for most of this century. This ballpark was so beloved by Pittsburghers that after the last game, fans ripped out the seats and took them home. Forbes Field opened in 1909, the same year the Pirates played the Detroit Tigers in the World Series. In that series, Honus Wagner of Pittsburgh faced off against Ty Cobb of Detroit. At one point Cobb attempted to steal second base from Wagner (after first admonishing, "Look out, Krauthead; I'm coming down"). The ball got to second well ahead of Cobb, giving Wagner enough time to prepare a forceful and strategic tag. Cobb lost several teeth and did not attempt to steal second again. The Pirates won that World Series—4 games to 3. This 1910 card commemorates that championship.

Since Forbes Field had the largest outfield in the majors, it was considered a pitcher's field because home runs were hard to come by. At the same time outfielders had more ground to cover and farther to throw to the infield, making it an ideal field for base hits. No Pirate ever pitched a no-hitter in Forbes Field. In 1947, the Pirates fenced in a portion of left field, thereby shortening it, to accommodate power-hitter Hank Greenberg. Visiting clubs dubbed it "Greenberg Gardens."

A souvenir card issued after the Pirates won the 1909 World Series. That's a red felt banner slightly obscuring the 1909 date. Note the "latest map of the world." Puzzle: Find Detroit.

In the top left of this view is the Carnegie Institute and Library. Across the bridge in the upper center is the entrance to Schenley Park and Phipps Conservatory (top right). To the left of the Conservatory, across the green expanse of Flagstaff Hill, is the Carnegie Institute of Technology, now Carnegie-Mellon University.

Webster Hall, one of the first high-rise buildings in Oakland, opened as a hotel/men's club, providing elegant lodgings for unmarried men of means. Membership did not require blue blood or sponsorship of a prominent member—only money. The club opened in 1926 and featured elaborate public rooms on the ground floor, a swimming pool and gymnasium with handball courts on the top two floors, and 400 bedrooms between. After brief popularity, management found there were not enough single men of means in Pittsburgh to fill the rooms. Webster Hall was converted into a hotel in 1931. Today the building serves as an apartment complex.

700 ROOMS FROM $2.00 TO $3.00 PER DAY

"Nothing gloomy or sordid," read an advertisement for this nighttime amusement park. Luna Park, located on South Craig/Bigelow Boulevard in Oakland, opened in 1905 with pavilions featuring architectural styles that were Byzantine, Japanese, Gothic, French Renaissance, Corinthian, and others. *The Pittsburgh Press* hailed it as "the grandest and most complete amusement and recreative resort between the two great oceans."

An interesting night at Luna Park, Pittsburg, Penn.

Besides vaudeville, roller coasters, and auto rides, Luna Park offered exotic forms of entertainment such as glass blowers, aerial artists, Geisha girls imported from Japan, Indian dances and ceremonies, gypsy camps, and all manner of "daring equestrians." The first incubator in the United States made its debut at Luna Park. This card shows the entrance to the park.

Although Luna Park was a nighttime entertainment center, it was easier to photograph it during the day. This card shows people gathered to watch "The Chutes," a roller coaster ride that patrons boarded at an entrance alongside the water to the left of the small bridge. The ride itself is out of the picture to the right.

LUNA PARK, PITTSBURGH, PA.   8069

This scene was the view from the top of The Chutes. Luna Park was Pittsburgh's most popular spot until 1907 when a lion from a lion-taming act escaped from its cage and mauled a customer to death. Profuse apologies from park officials and promises to diligently supervise the killer-animal exhibits failed to reassure the public. In 1919, the park was no longer listed in the City Directory.

Hugh Henry Brackenridge moved into the area in the 1780's when Pittsburgh was a fledgling town of 35 log houses, a few public buildings, and a fort. He helped establish the area's first newspaper, church, and school. The Pittsburgh Academy, founded in 1787 by an act of the Pennsylvania Legislature, had students ten years of age or younger. Tuition was three British pounds per annum, payable in advance.

In 1819, the Pennsylvania Legislature chartered The Western University of Pennsylvania. Funds for the old Academy were transferred to the new University. The school moved from one downtown location to another for years, chased by fires that were commonplace in the city back then. In the 1850's, the University erected a fireproof building on Grant Street and Ross where the City County Building is now. That building didn't burn down, but John Chislett's County Court House, a block away, did. The county asked the University to sell them the Ross Street building. The University moved across the river to Allegheny City. The buildings pictured in this card — Science Hall (left, 1889) and Main Hall (right, 1890) — were located on Perrysville Avenue. This location was so off the beaten path that the University was almost forgotten. Enrollment fell, donations fell, and key teachers left in disgust. The University had to move once again to survive.

Western University, ALLEGHANY, Pa.
Engineering Department, only

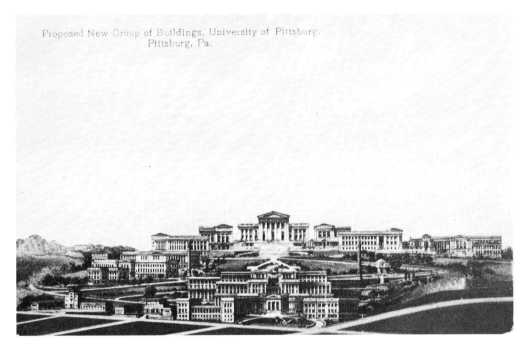

Proposed New Group of Buildings, University of Pittsburg, Pittsburg, Pa.

Schenley Farms (Oakland) was developing as Pittsburgh's new civic center. Many wealthy families were moving into this East area. Western University eyed some flat land across from Schenley Hotel known as Frick Acres, but Mr. Frick refused to sell. The only land the University could obtain was 45 acres of rough, nearly undeveloped land on the hill across from Frick Acres. A national competition to develop this site produced this winning design (1908) by the firm of Palmer and Hornbostel. The University planned to build Horbostel's Acropolis over a twenty-year period. Two of the buildings were erected — State Hall (now gone) and Thaw Hall. The Hornbostel design was abandoned after World War I. In 1909 Western University changed its name to University of Pittsburgh.

The prominent, wealthy trustees of the University of Pittsburgh believed in hiring the best possible candidate for the position of Chancellor. Once he was installed, however, the trustees wished him luck and advised him not to ask for money. Several of the University's trustees, being self-taught men, actually didn't believe in the value of higher education. Fortunately, Chancellor John Bowman was a man of vision who, like the businessmen who hired him, knew how to be persistent in pursuit of a goal. His special task in the 1920's was to expand the physical plant of the University. Bowman researched the space-per-student ratios of American schools and projected that Pitt would need 13 million cubic feet of space to meet the needs of students over the next ten years. Instead of the usual sprawl of low-level, ivy-covered buildings, Bowman envisioned a great stone tower of learning, reaching symbolically ever higher into the sky. It is said that the building we now call the Cathedral of Learning was inspired by music from Richard Wagner's *Die Walküre*. The whole city became involved with the building of this Gothic/Art Deco skyscraper. School children contributed "a dime a brick." It took eleven years to build and was considered an engineering marvel for its time.

Cathedral of Learning at Night, University of Pittsburgh, 50

Pittsburgh, Pa.   67419

St. Paul's Cathedral, Pittsburgh, Pa.

Pittsburgh became a Cathedral city by papal decree in 1843. St. Paul's Church, at Fifth and Grant Street, became the official Cathedral of the diocese. After one of the street hump removals, members had to climb steep wooden steps to get to the entrance of the Cathedral. When it caught fire in 1851, the fire department could not get water up to the building; it burned to the ground. Another St. Paul's Cathedral was built on the same spot in 1855. As Pittsburgh evolved into a major industrial center, the diocese moved to Oakland, selling their downtown property to Henry Clay Frick for $1,400,000. The third and current St. Paul's, pictured here, was designed by the Chicago firm of Egan and Prindeville, and was consecrated in 1906. Note the rural backdrop of the turn-of-the century Oakland setting. Today this Cathedral is surrounded by the congestion that the diocese originally sought to escape.

Homeopathic Hospital, Pittsburg, Pa.

Pittsburgh's Homeopathic Hospital incorporated in 1866, and its first buildings were downtown near First and Second Avenues and Cherry Way. The city employed the Homeopathic Hospital to treat city policemen, firemen, and other municipal workers. In 1910, the Homeopathic Hospital expanded by opening a larger facility on Center Avenue in Shadyside (shown here). Later, the American Medical Association launched an intense anti-Homeopathic campaign; the Homeopathic Hospital changed its name to Shadyside Hospital in 1938.

NEW WESTERN PENNSYLVANIA HOSPITAL, PITTSBURGH, PA.

West Penn Hospital was one of the first hospitals to open in the Pittsburgh area (1850). The first facility was located in Polish Hill. Civil War soldiers were treated there. This early hospital also treated many industrial accident victims from the nearby mills and railroads. In 1912 West Penn relocated to Bloomfield, opening the facility shown in this postcard. The various "forks" of the building housed the hospital, the nurses' dormitory, and a power plant and service structure.

Mud and Log Cabin, Penn Avenue, One of the City's first Homes, Pittsburgh, Pa.

This card shows a pioneer home from the early nineteenth century. This East Liberty dwelling was located near the heart of the business district.The mud was probably a mixture of clay, lime and horsehair. Regretfully, this relic of Pittsburgh's pioneer days is gone.

607 EAST LIBERTY PRESBYTERIAN CHURCH, PITTSBURGH, PA.

This Spanish Gothic church was built during the Depression with $4,000,000 donated by Richard Beatty Mellon and his wife. Less fortunate Pittsburghers, resentful of the Mellon millions, referred to this church as "the Mellon's fire escape." East Liberty became a suburb of Pittsburgh, although with its own office buildings, theaters, restaurants, and shops. The Pennsylvania Railroad also had a depot in East Liberty. This church with its 300-foot tower still stands.

Engine House No. 8, East Liberty, Pittsburg, Pa.

Back in the 1860's, "The Hook and Ladder" had two men, two horses, and a ladder wagon. The Engine House shown here was built in the late 1800's at the corner of Highland Avenue and Broad Street in East Liberty. Then, as now, men on call sometimes had time on their hands. This firehouse was built with an enclosed porch (decorated with flowers) for conversation and reading, a small library, and a space for exercising and conducting boxing matches. This old engine house is now gone.

Prominent East Enders sent their children to the Sterrett School, built near the turn of the century. The observatory dome housed a state-of-the-art John Brashear telescope donated by Henry Clay Frick, whose children attended the school.

At one time legitimate theater and vaudeville thrived in Pittsburgh. At the turn of the century downtown theaters entertained an average of 25,000 people a day. The motion picture was developed in Pittsburgh and first presented at The Nickelodeon on Smithfield Street. In 1897 The Nickelodeon (nickel: the price of a ticket; odeon: Greek for "theater") played continuously from 8 a.m. until midnight. By 1923 there were some 225 moving picture houses in Pittsburgh and its suburbs. One of the country's first drive-ins, The South Park, opened here in 1936. Drive-ins were so popular in this area that Pittsburgh came to be known as "The City of Drive-ins."

This card was issued by the Regent Theater and is one of five cards showing the lobby, auditorium, a fountain, and a wall-mounted work of art.

Beechwood Boulevard, showing Thaw Residence, Pittsburgh, Pa.

Pittsburgh's first millionaires row was in old Allegheny City. Later, many of Pittsburgh's wealthy re-located in Shadyside and Point Breeze, away from the sight, sound and smell of industrial Pittsburgh. This postcard shows the home of railroad and coal magnate William K. Thaw. Other East End aristocrats included George Westinghouse, H. J. Heinz, Richard Beatty Mellon, H. C. Frick (whose home, Clayton, is open to the public today), Thomas Armstrong (of the Armstrong Cork Company), Durbin Horne (of Joseph Horne's Department Store), and Andrew Carnegie's mother before her move to New York City.

R. B. Mellon Residence, 6500 Fifth Ave., Pittsburgh, Pa.

This Tudor-style East End Residence on Fifth Avenue, home of Richard Beatty Mellon, was designed by Alden and Harlow, architects of choice for many Pittsburgh millionaires. Completed in 1909, it featured 65 rooms and eleven baths. Most of the magnificent homes built by Pittsburgh's industrialists have been demolished, although several homes have been offered to the city as museums or for civic purposes. The Mellon home lasted 31 years before being demolished. The grounds were donated to the city for a park.

The Publishers Circulation Promotion Association put out this montage spotlighting the Superintendent of City Schools. The building identified as Carnegie Library is actually the Carnegie Institute, which housed the library and a great deal else. St. Paul's Cathedral is mentioned elsewhere in this book. Fifth Avenue High School, in the Hill District, was Pittsburgh's second high school. Some people considered the "typical East End residence" (Phipps-Braun House near Carnegie-Mellon University) to be the most beautiful mansion in the city, but it was demolished in the 1970's.

Just about every type of bridge has been constructed across Pittsburgh's waterways, including several stone-arch bridges. This one, built by the Pennsylvania Railroad between 1902-1903, has six masonry arches—one with a 100-foot span and five with 80-foot spans. Early in the century when this card was published, the Stone Arch Bridge crossed Silver Lake, which has since been drained.

ENTRANCE TO HIGHLAND PARK
3576   Pittsburgh, Pa.

Highland Park, the second park developed by E. M. Bigelow, is on land originally owned by Alexander Negley, who settled in the East Liberty Valley area after the Revolutionary. Caspar Negley sold some land to the city around 1871 for a second reservoir. The first reservoir, built on Grant Hill where the Frick Building now stands, had a walkway around it. A similar strolling place was built around the Highland reservoir. By 1879, it was pumping water to the Point, an engineering feat for the times. The rest of Highland Park was put together piecemeal by Mr. Bigelow, who padded his highway and waterworks budgets to create extra funds for park development.

The entrance to Highland Park, pictured here, was designed by Bigelow. The park opened in 1893.

Stephen Collins Foster was born in Pittsburgh on July 4, 1826, to a successful merchant family. Stephen's father, William Barclay Foster, became Mayor of Allegheny City. Young Stephen's musical talent was encouraged; while still in his teens, his melodies were famous throughout the country. But Foster consigned most of the rights to the sale of his music to the owners of the sheet music companies, making so little money that he was financially destitute much of his life. After his parents died, he could not support himself and took to drink. The composer of "Beautiful Dreamer," "Oh, Susanna," and "Jeannie With the Light Brown Hair" died in New York City at age 37 with 38 cents in his pocket.

This bronze monument by Guiseppe Moretti shows Foster composing "Uncle Ned," drawing inspiration from the man gently strumming his banjo. This sculpture was dedicated in Highland Park before a crowd of 50,000. Money for it was raised by donation, most of it in pennies donated by schoolchildren. Because it was vandalized in its isolated location, the monument was moved to its current place near the entrance to Schenley Park in the mid-1920's.

The Foster Monument, Highland Park, Pittsburg, Pa.

Lake Carnegie was originally created for the popular pastime of boating. The boathouse is gone now, and the lake has been filled in.

For a short time, there was a zoo at Schenley Park. With a gift from Christopher Magee, the city built this zoo in Highland Park, which opened in 1898, and the Schenley Park animals were transferred here. As the century progressed, zoos everywhere started adopting the popular "open space" approach of the San Diego Zoo. The Pittsburgh Zoo came to be seen as "a chicken wire menagerie suffering from concrete disease." Citizens organized, solicited donations, and floated bonds for a 75-acre, free-roaming habitat—The New Zoo—which is Highland Park's feature attraction.

Pittsburgh in perspective: old Onion Dome churches against the modern skyline.

At one time, Pittsburgh was so smokey from industrial pollution that street lights were left on all day. Businessmen took an extra shirt to work because the shirt they wore in the morning was too dirty to wear in the afternoon. Pittsburgh was described as "hell with the lid taken off."

Today, Pittsburgh is as close to heaven as a major metropolitan city can be. One writer for *The New Yorker* suggested that if Pittsburgh were in Europe, it would be considered an inland resort. In the 1980's, the Rand McNally Corporation rated Pittsburgh as the most livable city the U. S. This contemporary postcard shows how Pittsburgh looks today.

Bibliography

Alberts, Robert C. *The Good Provider*. Boston: Houghton Mifflin, 1973.

_____. *Pitt: The Story of the University of Pittsburgh, 1787-1987*. Pittsburgh: University of Pittsburgh Press, 1986.

Allegheny Centennial Committee. *The Story of Old Allegheny City*. Pittsburgh: Allegheny Centennial Committee, 1941.

Brown, Mark M., Lu Donnelly, and David G. Wilkins. *The History of the Duquesne Club*. Pittsburgh: Duquesne Club, 1989.

Craig, Neville B. *The History of Pittsburgh*. Pittsburgh: J. R. Weldin Co., 1917.

Gay, Vernon and Marilyn Evert. *Discovering Pittsburgh's Sculpture*. Pittsburgh: University of Pittsburgh Press, 1983.

Jacques, Charles J. *Goodbye, West View Park, Goodbye*. Pittsburgh: Amusement Park Journal, 1985.

_____. *Kennywood . . . Roller Coaster Capital of the World*. Vestal NY: The Vestal Press, Ltd., 1982.

Jacobs, Timothy. *The History of the Pennsylvania Railroad*. New York: Bonanza Books, 1988.

Johnson, Leland R. *The Davis Island Lock and Dam, 1870-1922*. Pittsburgh: U. S. Army Corps of Engineers, 1985.

Kidney, Walter C. *Landmark Architecture, Pittsburgh and Allegheny County*. Pittsburgh: Pittsburgh History and Landmarks Foundation, 1985.

Lorant, Stefan. *Pittsburgh: The Story of An American City*. Lennox, MA: Author's Edition, 1988.

Stevenson, W. H. and Burd S. Patterson, eds. *The Story of the Sesqui-Centennial*. Pittsburgh: R. W. Johnson Studios, 1910.

Toker, Franklin. *Pittsburgh: An Urban Portrait*. University Park and London: Pennsylvania State University Press, 1986.

Van Trump, James D. and Arthur P. Ziegler. *Landmark Architecture of Allegheny County, Pennsylvania*. (City) Pittsburgh History and Landmarks Foundation, 1967.

Van Trump, James D. *Life and Architecture in Pittsburgh*. Pittsburgh: Pittsburgh History and Landmarks Foundation, 1983.

_____. *Majesty of the Law: The Court Houses of Allegheny County*. Pittsburgh: Pittsburgh History and Landmarks Foundation, 1988.

Wall, Joseph Frazier. *Andrew Carnegie*. Pittsburgh: University of Pittsburgh Press, 1989.

INDEX

Acknowledgements

I am not one of those writers who love to write. Research is an endless joy, and there is nothing in the world more wonderful than holding a finished piece of writing in my hands. It's that part in between — the actual writing — I don't much care for. I'd first like to thank Gregory Weidner. Without his unending support this book would have taken at least ten more years to complete. In this same vein, I would like to thank Rick Corton, who has schemed with me on this book and assisted me on innumerable occasions. The order of the postcards was created by Rick in a seven-hour session, earning him a place of honor in the Friendship Hall of Fame.

I would also like to thank the Pittsburgh History and Landmarks Foundation, and Arthur Ziegler in particular, for allowing me access to the James D. Van Trump/Walter Kidney Library — a fine collection of rare and unusual books on the subject of Western Pennsylvania. The assistance offered me by the Carnegie Library of Pittsburgh cannot be measured. Without its Pennsylvania Room, much of our personal and social history would be lost. The librarians in the Pennsylvania Room have been helpful, patient, gracious, and even interested. After a while they must have become very tired of seeing my face, but I was always glad to see theirs.

Many people shared with me their memories of old Pittsburgh — in particular, Adam Lotz and Mary Wohleber. Adam was a bartender since Prohibition, living through a lot of history himself and serving men who lived back into the nineteenth century. Adam told wonderful stories about old Allegheny City and the working people of Pittsburgh that I had never heard or read before. He referred to himself as "just a man with an apron," but he was really a historian at heart. I miss him dearly. Mary Wohleber is one of Pittsburgh's greatest resources. Many Pittsbusrgh writers come to her to uncover Pittsburgh's unwritten history. Her knowledge and boundless enthusiasm are an inspiration. Thanks, Mary.

I would like to thank one of the fathers of Pittsburgh history, James D. Van Trump, for his knowledge and advice. He started the move to celebrate and appreciate Pittsburgh's architectural and social past. I would also like to thank George Swetnam, Robert C. Alberts, and Walter Kidney for the invaluable contributions they have made to the Pittsburgh bibliography.

Anyone who has researched Pittsburgh's history owes author Stephan Lorant a three-gun salute. Many critics regard his epic on Pittsburgh the finest book ever written on the history of a single city.

A special thanks to Dick Bowker, a postcard collector with his own book in the works, who mentioned my project to Harvey Roehl at Vestal Press. I would also like to thank Harvey, Grace Houghton, and Carol Brewer of Vestal Press for all of the work they have done on this project.

Several people were kind enough to give me permission to use postcards that are copyright protected; thanks to the H. J. Heinz Company for a 1960's advertising card, the Wonday Film Service for their postcard of the Civic Arena, Dale E. Röös for his card of St. Anthony's Chapel, Joel Levinson for the view of St. John the Baptist Church with the skyline in the background, and Ron Janoski for his postcard of the Point as it looks today. Also thanks to Dan Amerson for publishing Ron Janoski's card and for all his support.

Perhaps most important are my network of family and friends who have unconditionally supported me throught this project. I would like to thank my mother, Margret Ashworth; Roy and Kim Ashworth; Don and Dot Glusic; Chris Weidner and the whole Weidner clan, Bernie, Ben, Millie, Matt, Jackie, Dave, Eileen, Martin, Lowie, John, Becky. Thanks to Kathy Corton for helping to put my proposal together. I would like to thank Rosemary Reddinger, John Frank , Craig Melichar, Mike Masciantonio, Gil McAninch, Ken Boden, Doug and Deborah Gouge, Phil and Marcia Rostek, Vicci and Jack Kosko, Rich Liberto, and the Roads End crew, Avram, Lathe, Jim, Larry, Vicky, Kim, Nancy, Kate, Barb, Connie, Ken, and Walt.

Wherever I go in this city there are people who know about my postcard book. Invariably they ask, "How's the book coming?" Well, due largely to all of this support, it's coming along fine — it's done. Thank you!